SONG OF THE

SHEPHERD

Foundations OF THE Faith

Psalm 23

SONG OF THE SHEPHERD

Mark A. Tabb

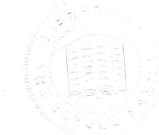

MOODY PRESS
CHICAGO

ISBN: 0-8024-6190-5

1 3 5 7 9 10 8 6 4 2

Printed in the United States of America

I lost a very special friend while writing this book.
Bill Todd, my father-in-law,
lost his battle with heart disease in March of 1998.
I dedicate this book to his memory.
He was a rare man of character.
I and many others sorely miss him.

CONTENTS

ACKNOWLEDGMENTS

$\mathcal{N}$ever before has the Lord so transformed my understanding of a passage of Scripture as He has during the months it took to write this book. Not only did He help me appreciate a wonderful poem I always took for granted, but He also allowed my family and me to see the power of this song through some very dark trials. I come away from this project with a renewed sense of awe for God and the ancient king through whom the Lord communicated this song of His great love.

I want to thank Jim Bell of Moody Press for giving me the privilege of writing this book. I also want to thank Bill Soderberg of Moody for his patience and Julie Ieron for her encouragement. Thank you as well to my editor, Cheryl Dunlop. It was a joy to work with you once again. It is an honor to be able to contribute to the ministry of Moody Press.

I want to also say a very special word of thanks to Mike Becraft. If not for Mike this book would not have been written. His encouragement and enthusiasm for this project spurred me on when I was ready to give up. Thank you as well to my church family at the First Baptist Church of Knightstown for your prayers and support during the trials my family and I faced during the writing of this book.

Introduction

BACKGROUND

NOISE

I hate to brag, but I am a musical genius. My voice has the rare quality of being able to sound exactly like most popular singers. In fact, if the radio is turned up loud enough, you cannot tell whether it is me or Memorex. Alone on a stage with a microphone in front of me my voice makes children cry and adults cover their ears. But in the car with the windows down and the radio up, I sound pretty terrific, if I do say so myself.

And my range is—not that I'm bragging—quite remarkable. My parents tortured me as a child by making me listen to those old K-Tel "Hits of the Fifties" eight tracks as we traveled. As a result, I can hit all the low notes with Elvis in "Blue Christmas." Because I grew up in Oklahoma, *the* home of country music, I can keep up with Willie and Waylon and the boys. A member of the high school class of 1979, I know all the words to all the hits of all the supergroups of the seventies. Not to be left behind by my three daughters, I can sing both versions of

Jesus Freak and (this is remarkable) I understand the words to all of the Newsboys' songs. From Elvis to alternative Christian rock, I can sing them all.

Because I possess such rare musical talent, I constantly hit the scan button while driving, searching for songs I know, songs I can sing real loud. One day while traveling up the Ventura Highway (. . . *in the springtime . . . do da do do*) a song from my teenage years came on an oldies station. Like any good child of the seventies, I cranked the volume and sang along. I had not heard the song in more than fifteen years, yet I remembered the words. Halfway through the song I stopped singing and started listening. Back in my high school days I was clueless as to what songs said. My friends and I just wanted something that, in the words of Dick Clark, had a beat we could dance to (or drive to). Driving down the highway on this afternoon I heard the message behind the words. I was shocked by it, and shocked by how oblivious to it I had been all those years ago.

I was oblivious because so much of the music you and I listen to is little more than background noise to the rest of our lives. It is always there, but we never really listen. A similar fate often befalls the Twenty-third Psalm. From funeral services to disaster movies, David's little masterpiece turns up everywhere in a variety of forms. When I searched the World Wide Web for references to the Twenty-third Psalm I found over four *million* matches. *Four million!* Its simplicity makes it easy to personalize . . . and trivialize. There is a Twenty-third Psalm for everything from students (the Lord is my shepherd, I shall not flunk), to mathematicians (the Lord is my thesis adviser, I shall not err), to computers (the Lord is my programmer,

I shall not crash), and computer geeks (the modem is my shepherd. . . . It makes me connect to alt.green.pastures).

The song of the shepherd penned by David nearly three thousand years ago has grown so popular that we all know it, but none of us hear it. Why listen? We know what it has to say. And it is so upbeat that everyone enjoys it. So much of the Bible talks about death and deliverance and judgment, but not the Twenty-third Psalm. Other psalms lament recent tragedies, but the twenty-third assures us that God will protect us. Blessing and sunshine and goodness and love, the song is the ultimate pick-me-up. Not even death can dampen its mood. The final refrain lifts our eyes to heaven with the words, *and I will dwell in the house of the Lord forever!*

The one thing we like best of all about the psalm is that it gives us all of the above without making any demands on us. There aren't any references to sin or guilt or any of those negatives that turn us off to organized religion. God comes across as a God of love, not a rule maker with narrow guidelines for entrance into His kingdom. When the Twenty-third Psalm is separated from the rest of Scripture (as it is in popular usage), it presents us with a God whose arms are open to all comers, no questions asked. *The Lord is my shepherd, and He can be yours as well.* Our approach is so sentimental and romanticized that the psalm is treated more like the inside of a greeting card than inspired Scripture.

It is time for us to stop, turn up the volume, and listen. We have missed the point of David's song. The song of the shepherd is about more than comfort in times of sorrow. Within its words is a challenge to you and me to live a different kind of life. These familiar words written nearly three thousand years ago by Israel's shepherd king call us to live a life of total dependence upon the Lord.

To fully appreciate the call of the Twenty-third Psalm, we need to listen to its words as spoken by its original writer. The song is so personal that we sometimes forget that we are not the "my" in its words. The one who said, "The Lord is my shepherd," was David, the second king over Israel, the man entrusted with the job of being the shepherd over the nation of Israel nearly three thousand years ago. He was a man unlike any who came before or since. God Himself testified of David that he was a man after God's own heart. His reign became both the standard by which every other king was measured and the hope of those waiting for the Messiah, the son of David.

When David came to power, the tribes of Israel were in chaos. After the death of Saul, the first king, the northern tribes pledged their allegiance to Ish-Bosheth, one of Saul's descendants, while the southern tribe of Judah anointed David as king. Seven years of civil war followed until David was finally able to unite the kingdom under his reign. With a stroke of diplomatic genius, he then conquered the city of Jerusalem from the Jebusites and created a new capitol for the nation, a capitol that belonged neither to the north or the south. For the next thirty-two years David ushered in a period of peace and prosperity unlike any the nation had ever dreamed of. All of the promises God made through Moses about the land of Canaan finally came true. The Philistines were subdued, surrounding nations paid tribute to Israel's throne, and the borders of Israel's influence stretched from the river of Egypt to the Euphrates. David was more than a king, he was a national hero, the greatest man the nation ever produced.

This same man wrote, "The Lord is my shepherd, I shall not be in want. He makes me lie down in green pastures." To David, these were more than sentimental words describing God's love and compassion. They were a bold statement of dependence and humility before the Lord. With these words he was in effect saying that in comparison to God, the great king was nothing more than a helpless lamb before a shepherd. David knew who had placed him on the throne. He knew who had defeated the giant Goliath and all the other foes he faced during his lifetime. David never forgot that the Lord was the true King of the nation, the one true Shepherd under whose authority David served. His confession was a statement of true humility.

Humility is an indispensable element of faith. Without it, faith degenerates into nothing more than positive thinking or a magic formula by which we try to wrench favors from the hand of God. Positive thinking cannot save a soul, nor does God respond to the reciting of meaningless prayers and formulas. The first step toward life as a sheep before the Shepherd is the realization of the greatness of God and the worthlessness of our own selves. We must begin with the confession that we are sinners totally incapable of saving ourselves. This goes far beyond belief in a higher power. It plunges us totally and completely on the mighty, Sovereign Lord of the universe.

Paul had this in mind when he described true Christians with these words: "For it is we who are the circumcision, we who worship by the Spirit of God, who glory in Christ Jesus, and who put no confidence in the flesh" (Philippians 3:3).

Paul then went on to describe why he of all people had reason to place confidence in his own abilities and accomplishments. But he concluded the matter by saying, "I consider everything a loss compared to the surpassing greatness of knowing Christ Jesus my Lord" (Philippians 3:8). These words came from a man whose education approached the modern equivalent of a Ph.D., a missionary who took the gospel around the world, a man who penned thirteen books of the Bible. Yet Paul understood that faith means humbling ourselves under the mighty hand of God. David echoes Paul's words when he confesses his utter dependence on his Shepherd, the one true God. The Twenty-third Psalm calls us to do the same.

Claiming the Lord as our Shepherd also means we will be faithful to Him alone. David penned the words of the Twenty-third Psalm in the middle of a time in Israel's history when the people were in constant flux as to which of the pantheon of ancient gods they would serve. Between Israel's birth as a nation under Moses and the reign of David, judges ruled the nation under the authority of God. Although the period started out with such promise under Moses the lawgiver and Joshua his successor, the people of Israel soon began to copy the practices of the nations they had displaced in the land of Canaan. The writer of the book of Judges described it as a time when everyone did what was right in their own eyes. This was especially true in the area of religion. Altars to Baal, the god of the Canaanites, and Asherah, the fertility goddess, had sprung up on high places everywhere. In addition, the Lord's chosen people served the gods of the Philistines and the Amorites as well as the gods of every other nation around them. Each time the people would turn to an idol, the Lord would send some sort of judgment to call them back to Himself. Israel's history during this time is a yo-yo cycle of fidelity to the God of Israel and any other god that happened to catch their eye.

Once God gave Israel a king, the cycle did not stop. Solomon, David's son and successor to the throne, erected altars to Molech and Chemosh, detestable gods of the Ammonites and the Moabites. He also reintroduced the worship of Asherah with all of its blatant sexuality. This came at the end of Solomon's life, after he built the fabulous temple of the Lord in Jerusalem in fulfillment of his father's dream. Idolatry remained an integral part of Israel's history until God sent them into exile in Babylon. Yet they never completely abandoned the Lord. The ancient Israelites would serve the Lord while also participating in the deviant sexual practices that were used in the worship of Baal and Asherah. People would pray to the one true God while also sacrificing their children to Molech, the fire god.

In the middle of all of this, David confesses, "The *Lord* is my shepherd." The word *Lord* is actually the name of God, the name Yahweh. Those who listened to this song at the time of its writing understood that the king was professing his loyalty to Yahweh as opposed to some other rival god. In this way David's words sound very much like those of Joshua who declared:

> Choose for yourselves this day whom you will serve, whether the gods your forefathers served beyond the

River, or the gods of the Amorites, in whose land you are living. But as for me and my household, we will serve the Lord [Yahweh]. (Joshua 24:15)

We live in a time when idolatry is more subtle, but we are still faced with the same choice David called the people of Israel to make. There are some actual false gods that have made their way to the Western world by way of the New Age movement. But for the most part, we must choose between the one true God and impostors that we sometimes do not recognize as gods. A god is anything we focus our attention upon and adore as precious in our sight. These include the god of wealth, the god of pleasure, the god of sensuality, and in Indiana, the god of basketball. When we stop and take inventory, we find we too are up against a pantheon of suitors trying to win our devotion.

David's words in the Twenty-third Psalm call us to make a choice. We cannot sing the song of the shepherd and claim it as our own when we place our own careers above the Lord. Reciting "though I walk through the valley of the shadow of death I will fear no evil for you are with me" during a time of trial is nothing more than a sick joke when we consistently skip church to watch our favorite teams play on Sunday. As we explore the Twenty-third Psalm, we will find that it does not call us to keep all of our rival interests in balance. It calls us to make a choice. Which God will we serve? David makes it clear that he has already made his choice. He calls us to do the same.

Some commentators believe David wrote the Twenty-third Psalm late in life. They draw a picture of the old king sitting in his palace, thinking back to the carefree days of his youth when he sat on a hill watching his father's sheep. I don't think that was what David had in mind as he wrote these words. It wasn't during his time as a shepherd that he learned to depend on God. Rather he learned those lessons after his shepherd days ended, as he waited for God's promises to come true.

When David was an adolescent, still living at home, still caring for his father's sheep, an old prophet came to his home. The prophet poured oil upon David's head and proclaimed, "You are God's choice to be the next king of Israel." There was only one problem: Israel already had a king, and he had other plans for his successor. From that moment forward David had to believe God for that which seemed impossible. Shortly after Samuel the prophet anointed him as king, David stood on a battle-field face-to-face against the champion of the Philistine army. Goliath was over nine feet tall with many victories under his belt. David was little more than an adolescent. The Philistine champion was decked out in full armor, with a sword, spear, and shield at his side. David was dressed in his shepherd's clothes armed only with his shepherd's weapons, a sling and a stick. Against all odds, David won the battle by trusting in the Lord.

His victory did not bring the throne closer to him. Instead, it made the thought of becoming king even more remote. Saul, the sitting king of Israel, set out on a campaign to kill David. He was jealous of the accolades the crowds poured out on the young man. Even after David became the king's son-in-law, he was not safe. Saul hunted him like a dog across the hills of Israel. David lost everything to Saul's jealousy: his wife, his position in the nation, his hope, everything. He reached his lowest point when he was forced to hide in one of the cities of the Philistines pretending to be a madman.

During this time of running David composed another psalm. Listen to the way it begins; "I will extol the Lord at all times; his praise will always be on my lips. My soul will boast in the Lord; let the afflicted hear and rejoice" (Psalm 34:1–2). Even when he had nothing, even when everyone had abandoned him and he had to pretend to be insane to save his own life, David knew that the Lord would never let him down. To say he knew what it meant to live by faith is a gross understatement. As he boldly proclaimed, "The Lord is my shepherd, I shall not be in want," he knew what it meant to wonder where his next meal would come from. The lessons he learned while running for his life and hiding in caves spill out in the song he penned.

The fifty-six Hebrew words that are the Twenty-third Psalm are much more than religious background noise. They call all of us to live by simple trust in God. The call of the Twenty-third Psalm is the call to a life of dependence upon the Lord. In the pages that follow we will explore each line of the song of the shepherd and find a different aspect of what it means to follow the Lord as our Shepherd. Listening to the call is not optional: It is the only way to live a life that pleases God. Our first step brings us face-to-face with an unpleasant truth. In fact, the opening line of the song can be downright disturbing.

Chapter One

THE LORD IS

MY SHEPHERD

$\mathcal{I}$t is insulting. I don't know how else to describe it. The nerve, the absolute nerve, to call me a thing like this. At first I didn't mind. The idea seemed novel, comforting . . . but not anymore. The more I think about it, the madder I get. No one has the right to slander me like this. No one. I am not, I repeat am not, like one of those helpless, stupid creatures. I am not . . . a sheep.

At least, I do not want to be.

Who would?

Sheep are not fearless, rugged creatures whose character inspires us to greatness. They are passive, dependent blobs of wool. I do not want to put myself in their company. I prefer to be compared to our national symbol, the eagle. Eagles are strong, resilient, independent. That's what I want to be, an eagle that soars above the winds of adversity.

But the Bible never calls you and me eagles. It says we are sheep.

No one uses the sheep as its national symbol, not even New Zealand, which has more sheep than people. Sheep are everything we do not want to be. They are notorious followers. If one member of a flock decides to start running toward the highway, everyone else takes off after him. None of them knows why they are running. The herd instinct takes over, the urge to follow, and off they go. They will mindlessly follow anything that catches their attention.

They are also helpless. Carnivores love sheep. The sight of a sheep away from the protection of the shepherd says "Dinner is served" to a hungry wolf. Wolves never fear a counterattack when they make their way into the flock. They know that the biggest, baddest sheep in the flock can do very little to defend itself in case of attack. Even if a sheep ducks its head and charges, a hard head cannot stop sharp teeth and murderous skill.

And sheep are hardheaded. The wild ones of the species, the bighorned mountain variety, continually run around banging heads with one another. Apparently it really impresses the lady sheep. I think it would give me a headache.

Maybe the reason banging heads does not give sheep a headache is that their cranial cavity has a lot of extra space. Sheep are not known for their intelligence. Before you accuse me of species bias, consider one of the more peculiar habits of sheep. Adult sheep will, from time to time, lie down and roll over on their backs. My cocker spaniel lies on her back, but sheep are not as agile as cocker spaniels. When a sheep rolls onto its back, it is physically unable to roll back over. Shepherds refer to this situation as a cast sheep. Unless the shepherd rolls it back over, internal gases will build up and the sheep will die. That is correct. Sheep will die if they lie on their backs, yet they continue doing so. This is obviously not a highly intelligent animal. This is not the sort of animal I want to be identified with. An animal so helpless. So stupid.

And throughout the Bible God calls you and me sheep.

The Twenty-third Psalm reaffirms our "sheepness" in its first line, "The Lord is my shepherd." Usually we think of this phrase as a beautiful, inspirational affirmation of God's love for us. And it is. But listen closely to what it says about you and me. The Lord is my Shepherd. Shepherds work with sheep. All day, every day, a shepherd's task is to watch over the helpless flock. If the Lord is *our* Shepherd then that makes us . . . sheep, in all of their infamy. I don't know what offends me more, the fact that the Lord calls us sheep or the knowledge that when He does He is exactly right.

Before we can ever begin to understand the magnitude of the promises of the Twenty-third Psalm, we must first come to grips with the proper position for us to take before the Lord our Shepherd. The process is both humbling and liberating. The first step is admitting we are sheep. Like it or not, we bear a strong family resemblance. We share their natural tendency to follow. Very few among us are natural born leaders, and often the leaders among us are like those sheep running toward the highway. Some member of the human flock will take off in some direction and all of us will fall in line behind.

I tried to dispute this fact in my mind the other day, and I did a pretty good job—until I got out of bed and looked around. As my daughters got ready for school, I looked closely at their clothes. The legs of their jeans absolutely had to be a certain width (at the time of this writing wider is better, but who knows what the situation will be six months from now), and the shirts looked exactly like the shirts everyone else in school wears. They won't be caught dead in the discount-store shoes we used to get by with in their younger days. Now their feet have to be covered with Nikes or Airwalks or whatever everyone else is wearing these days. Before I could become too disgusted with my sheep-ish daughters, I looked in the mirror. The look of the flock stared back at me.

If this were all a matter of style the situation would not be too bad. But the human species regularly surrenders its will to someone else in order to run after the flock. Right and wrong depend on the latest poll. Whatever everyone else thinks or does is what we think and do. We simply fall in line, running along with the rest of the flock wherever our woolly little legs may carry us.

Like sheep, we are also helpless. A different breed of carnivore stalks us—hunters hungry not for flesh and blood but for our hearts and minds. Human beings are especially vulnerable to spiritual predators who offer false paths to forgiveness and hope. I am constantly amazed at the absurd notions educated people will believe in their quest for hope in this world. One group in California recently purchased a large field to serve as a landing field for a fleet of flying saucers. The friendly visitors from another dimension are set to arrive at the dawn of the new millennium. The true believers who are waiting for E.T.'s arrival are not burned-out hippies from the sixties. Most are professionals or blue-collar workers, all desperate to find something more in life. The Bible calls them sheep without a shepherd, lost on a hillside, about to be devoured.

We have a lot of other common characteristics with sheep. Like sheep we constantly go astray. Somehow we arrived at the mistaken notion that we do not need anyone, when in fact our independence leads only to death. Once we wander away, we are too hardheaded to try to find our way back. Romans 3:11 tells us that human sheep never seek God. He has to search for us or we will die in the wilderness. All of this suggests we have another common bond with sheep; like them, we are not particularly bright. We do not learn from the mistakes of the past but constantly repeat them as we attempt to survive on our own apart from the shepherd.

But we can't survive on our own. We are sheep in need of a shepherd. Thankfully, God is willing to take the job.

Sheep need a shepherd. We need the Lord. When David penned these words, "the Lord is my shepherd," he spoke of a choice that God made long ago. Most of us have grown so accustomed to the concept of the Lord's loving care of us that we forget that He did not have to take the job of shepherding such a hardheaded flock. God is under no obligation to care for us or lead us or protect us. That He would want to do any of these things should come as a complete surprise. Why would He want the headaches, the heartaches? Why would He extend His hand toward those who have already slapped Him away in the past? Like sheep, we have all gone astray. We all ran away from the safety of His pen long ago, and we deserve whatever fate befalls us. But God chose to rescue us and take us into His care.

The thirty-fourth chapter of Ezekiel paints a desperate picture of the human race. Ezekiel describes us as sheep who have suffered under shepherds that used the flock for their own personal gain. These shepherds slaughtered the choice animals, ignored those who wandered away, and allowed the remaining animals to become dinner for all the wild animals. Ezekiel captured the essence of the plight of all of mankind: lost, helpless, hopeless, desperate with no one to turn to. As the Lord surveyed this situation, He made this declaration:

> I myself will search for my sheep and look after them. As a shepherd looks after his scattered flock when he is with them, so will I look after my sheep. I will rescue them from all the places where they were scattered on a day of clouds and darkness. . . . I myself will tend my sheep and have them lie down, declares the Sovereign Lord. . . . I will shepherd the flock with justice. (Ezekiel 34:11–12, 15–16)

The Lord looked down from heaven and saw the plight we had brought upon ourselves. The sound of our bleating in fear and frustration moved His heart to act. But He had always planned to act. Long before we first ran away He knew what would have to be done for any of the flock to be saved. Our cries rang out as we received exactly what we deserved. Yet the Lord in His great mercy and grace chose to come down and rescue us. He chose to become our Shepherd.

I need to be reminded of this fact on a regular basis. Otherwise I start taking the Lord's loving care for granted.

I also need to be reminded of the price He paid to make me a part of His flock. Human sheep do not come cheap, not because we are so valuable but because the plight we were in was so desperate. God chose to become our Shepherd, and He did so at the cost of the life of His Son. All we like sheep had gone astray, and the Lord brought us back by laying our sin and guilt on His Son on the cross (Isaiah 53:6). The Lord is my Shepherd, but I do not deserve the privilege of being a part of His flock.

As I said earlier, before we can appreciate the depth of the promises of this familiar psalm, we must first come to grips with our sheepness. Only then can we understand the price the Lord paid to make us a part of His flock. We must also see our sheepness before we can take the next step to understand what it means that He is our Shepherd.

Caring for sheep was hard work in the ancient Near East. Israel's summers are long and dry. A year's worth of rain falls between the months of November and April. Even then the total rainfall pales in comparison to what we receive in Indiana: the central region of Israel receives between twelve and eighteen inches of rain per year. All of this made the ancient shepherd's job very taxing. Grass on the hillsides withers and disappears by mid-summer. Palestinian streams stay dry for up to six months at a time, making water difficult to find. In addition, in David's time the hills were full of wildlife, including lions and bears.

If the sheep are to survive in such a hostile environment, the shepherd must take complete control over the flock. He never polls the sheep to see what they want to do. The shepherd makes every decision for the flock. He leads it where he knows it needs to go; he chooses the hillside with the best pasture; he finds the streams with the best water. When predators invade, he springs into action and defends the flock. The life of every lamb is in his hand. Each sheep is totally dependent upon him for its survival.

When we wax eloquent about the Lord being our Shepherd, we need to understand that this is no sentimental concept designed to move our emotions. King David understood the absolute control shepherds exercise over their flocks. When he wrote, "The Lord is my shepherd," he was confessing that God was the sovereign Lord over his life and that of everyone else who names the name of the Lord. David admitted what the psalm calls us all to understand. We don't manage our own destinies; we are not in control of our lives. We don't even own ourselves. You and I belong to the Lord. He owns us; He is Lord over us. Like a shepherd, He decides what is best for us.

The fortieth chapter of the book of Isaiah paints a picture of God's absolute supremacy over the world. Before Him all men are like grass, and their glory is like the flowers that fade under the summer sun. All of the waters of the earth fit in the hollow of His hand, and the vast space of the universe is a mere handbreadth to Him. Isaiah tells us that God's wisdom exceeds our wildest imagination. In comparison to Him, all of the nations are like a drop of water in a bucket. Nothing compares to Him, in heaven or on earth. He alone is the majestic, sovereign Lord. He alone is God.

In the middle of this picture Isaiah includes these words:

> See, the Sovereign Lord comes with power, and his arm rules for him. See, his reward is with him, and his recompense accompanies him. He tends his flock like a shepherd . . . he gently leads those that have young. (Isaiah 40:10–11)

Picture this. God in all His splendor and power and majesty invades the affairs of men. He comes to take control. All of the earth trembles as He makes His way across the earth.

When we think about the lordship of our Shepherd, this is the picture we need to keep in mind. He is no young shepherd boy on the side of a Judean hill, stuck with the task of taking care of some mangy old sheep. The Lord who is our Shepherd is the King of kings and Lord of lords. In light of who He is, can we as sheep do anything less than humbly submit ourselves to Him?

One line in the fortieth chapter of Isaiah jumps out at me: "He gathers the lambs in his arms and carries them close to his heart" (v. 11). The rest of the chapter shows God in His awesome might, a picture that strikes fear in the stoutest of hearts. But as He scoops us up in His arms we see the gentle love the Lord has for us. He leads and cares for us with a love we cannot fully comprehend.

Jesus filled in the details of the greatness of His love for His sheep when He told His disciples, "I am the good shepherd; I know my sheep and my sheep know me . . . and I lay down my life for the sheep" (John 10:14–15). Growing up in the suburbs, the closest I ever came to seeing a shepherd in action came through watching Saturday morning cartoons. Jesus, however, knew sheep. He grew up in the home of a carpenter, but He lived in an area with plenty of sheep, and He understood the shepherd and sheep dynamic. He drew on this as He said, "I am the Good Shepherd." Like the word picture in Isaiah, Jesus used this imagery to show His tender care for us. To Him, we are more than blobs of wool out in a field. He knows us by name. Imagine, with nearly six billion people on the planet, and many millions of born-again Christians, He never loses track of one of us. John 10:3 tells us the Shepherd "calls his own sheep by name and leads them out." He loves us individually.

When He calls, we know it. Middle Eastern shepherds lead their flocks by singing or whistling. Every shepherd's song is unique. Somehow, sheep are able to distinguish the sound of their shepherd's voice even among a crowd. Once they hear it they take off after him. Jesus said in John 10:4–5 that His sheep follow Him because they know His voice. His sheep will not follow a stranger because the pitch of his voice is all wrong, and the song is not the same. Our relationship with our Lord, our Shepherd, is so personal that we know the sound of His voice. Our ears should strain to hear His call. This is not the picture of frightened sheep cowering in a corner lest the shepherd smack them on the head with his staff. The relationship we have with our Shepherd is intimate. He knows us, and we long to know Him more.

Most ordinary shepherds had limits as to how far they would go to protect the sheep. Not our Shepherd. Jesus told His disciples, "I am the good shepherd. The good shepherd lays down his life for the sheep" (John

10:11). The day He went to the cross He proved that these were more than words. The only way He could rescue His sheep was to die in their place. No one forced Him to do this. He did it because He loves His sheep, including you and me.

Like it or not, you and I are sheep. It is nothing to be proud of. I wish the Lord would have used a different analogy, but this one fits too well. It deflates our pride and exposes our independence as a myth. Sheep. Hardheaded, stubborn, helpless sheep. And He is the Shepherd. Powerful, mighty, sovereign; loving, gentle, tender. This is more than a comforting notion. It is a call to a changed way of life.

Living as a sheep before the Great Shepherd demands that we humble ourselves before the Lord. We cannot claim this psalm as our own until we are willing to stop baaing orders at Him and complaining about the pasture He has selected. As long as we run around thinking we are in charge, the opening line of the Twenty-third Psalm is nothing more than inspirational poetry. If we listen closely, we will hear these words calling us to admit we are sheep and to humble ourselves before the Shepherd.

These words also call us to live a life of total dependence upon the Lord. This does not come naturally for most of us. We have everything that we could possibly need at our fingertips. Stretching the budget between paydays may call for some financial gymnastics, but American Christians rarely go to bed with an empty stomach. We complain about our mortgage payments, but we have roofs over our heads. Not only is depending on someone else for everything unnatural, but we even have difficulty seeing the need to do so.

Living as a sheep before the Shepherd calls us to live a life that is out of the ordinary. Depending upon the Lord means placing everything that we have at His disposal. We must surrender to Him the ownership of all that we claim as our own. Putting dependence into action also means our first line of defense when problems strike is prayer, not worry.

Every single day of our lives will change when we begin to live as sheep before the Shepherd. No longer will we plot out our own course. Wherever He leads, we go. His will takes precedence over our agendas. Every day we must decide to depend on Him, and not ourselves. Only then will these words mean anything at all; only then can we truly say, "The Lord is my Shepherd. No more wandering. No more choosing my own way. The Shepherd is calling; I must follow."

That's what sheep are supposed to do.

Chapter Two

I SHALL NOT

BE IN WANT

We come into the world making demands. It's not that we are hard to please, but there are a few things we need. Once those basic needs are satisfied, we can relax, enjoy life, and be content. As infants we don't want much: a little something to eat, a warm place to sleep, lots of love, and an occasional dry diaper. And by the way, we would like that little something to eat about every two or three hours, even in the middle of the night. One more thing, not to be pushy, but we need to feel the love we desire. Just hold us, and rock us, and play with us, and stay where we can see you at all times, and we will be content. Make sure the diaper stays dry.

As we grow older our needs grow with us. Between the ages of two and twelve we still don't want much. All we need is a little something to eat, a warm place to sleep, lots of love, and clothes to wear. A few toys would make life a little more enjoyable, especially if one of them happened to be a Totally Hair Barbie® or a sixty-four bit

Nintendo® system or a mountain bike. And could you throw in a Barbie dream house and maybe a Barbie Ferrari? And if she's going to have a house and a car she really needs a few friends—that is, if it's not too much trouble? While we're at it, our own rooms would be nice (away from our little brother), and our own television and phone line could really come in handy for someone approaching those teenage years. And there's still the matter of clothes. All we need is something to wear to school, but it needs to be something in style. Not that we are ungrateful, but could we get our clothes from the mall this year rather than the discount store?

In our teen years and into adulthood we still don't need much. Basically, all we want is all we have ever wanted: a little something to eat, a warm place to sleep, lots of love, and clothes to wear. We simply need to upgrade a few of the items we already have. The Nintendo needs to be upgraded to a multimedia notebook computer, the mountain bike to a car, and the Barbie dream house for a real house. After everything is upgraded, we can relax, enjoy life, and be content.

Except now that we are adults we need to update our wardrobe and the car has a few too many miles on it and doctor bills keep piling up and the furniture is starting to get a little ratty and the refrigerator is making a strange noise and really should be replaced and then there's ... The list never seems to end. We don't mean to be demanding, but life is an expensive proposition.

At least we know that we don't face it alone. *The Lord is my shepherd*. What a relief. With the Lord on our side we know that He will take care of us, His precious flock. As a result, *I shall not be in want*. We don't need to worry about mortgages or soaring interest rates or the Consumer Price Index. We're taken care of. As the psalmist said elsewhere, "I was young and now I am old, yet I have never seen the righteous forsaken or their children begging bread" (Psalm 37:25). Like a good shepherd, the Lord will provide everything that we need. Now what did I do with that list?

Unfortunately, this is the way we usually approach the second line of the Twenty-third Psalm. Our ears hear these words as a promise from God to care for our every need. (And we do have a lot of needs, and a lot of wants we manage to reclassify as needs, not that we mean to be demanding.) But David's words do not come to us in the form of a promise. In the original text the first two lines of the psalm are comprised of only four words. Unlike most English translations, the words are not neatly divided in the Hebrew text into two distinct lines. They stand together as one sentence, one statement of faith. The best translation, one that communicates David's core idea, is, "The Lord is my shepherd; *I don't need anything else.*"

This statement affirms what we too often forget in our never-ending maze of wants and desires: When we have the Lord we have everything we need. I shall not be in want, for I do not want anything else besides Him. And I do want Him—all of us do, whether we realize it or not. As human beings, our greatest need is to know the Lord. We can deny it, hide it, suppress it, or try to substitute something for it, but deep within each one of us lies a hunger that can only be satisfied with the Lord Himself. Until we have Him we can never be satisfied, but with Him we need nothing else.

The problem with the above statement is that the

vast majority of people who cross our paths every day do not think of God as a need. If they did they would look for Him, but no one does. David himself wrote of the human race, "The Lord looks down from heaven on the sons of men to see if there are any who understand, any who seek God. All have turned aside. . . . there is no one who does good, not even one" (Psalm 14:2–3). Paul summarized David's thoughts with the statement, "There is no one who understands, no one who seeks God" (Romans 3:11). If a burning desire dwells deep within the heart of every individual, a desire that only God can satisfy, our behavior betrays us. For most people God is an afterthought or a means to an end. We want Him to make life more bearable, to help us feel better about ourselves. He can give us love, and we like that. But to call Him our greatest desire? That may be stretching things a bit.

Yet our inability to find satisfaction through any earthly pursuit tells us that something is missing from our lives, something we cannot live without. Solomon wrote in Ecclesiastes 3:11, "[God] has also set eternity in the hearts of men; yet they cannot fathom what God has done from beginning to end." This verse describes both the burning desire and the inevitable frustration that fills our hearts. We long for something more than the temporal world can offer. Our minds are made in such a way that they constantly race past the events of our lives in a search for some meaning, some way of making sense of it all. Deep within us lies an insatiable desire to know how things work, why they happen, and what role we play in it all. Thus, a sunset is more than a sunset. The artist tries to reproduce its dazzling array of color, lovers sit and soak in the beauty of the moment, and the scientist sets out to uncover the mystery of the fragile relationship between our planet and a burning ball of gas.

Sunsets must be more than sunsets, and life must be more than life. We are made to look, made to wonder, made to long for more. The Bible never comes out and tells us that what we long for is God. Nor, for that matter, does the Bible ever explain the mystery of the existence of God. The first words of the book of Genesis simply state, "In the beginning God." He is, and everything owes its existence to Him. In the same way, from Genesis to Revelation the Lord makes the promise, "I will be your God and you will be My people." He never tells us why this is a good deal for us. We are never told, "And this is what you really want." No one has to tell us—we already know it to be true. Eternity burns within our hearts. When our blinded eyes are finally opened to see the glory of the Lord, we realize that He is the One we have been longing for all along.

Our problem is not that our desires for everything else the world has to offer are too strong. Rather, our desires are too weak. C. S. Lewis said it best,

> We are half-hearted creatures, fooling about with drink and sex and ambition when infinite joy is offered to us, like an ignorant child who wants to go on making mud pies in a slum because he cannot imagine what is meant by the offer of a holiday at the sea. We are far too easily pleased.[1]

The Lord Himself through His Holy Spirit makes us dissatisfied with all we want in order that we might see the one thing we truly desire.

A parched woman near the Samaritan town of Sychar felt this dissatisfaction the day she crossed paths with Jesus. Day after day she made the same trip to the same well to draw the same water. One day her routine was broken. A Jewish man spoke to her, asking her for a drink of water. Before she knew it, this Man offered her the water she had searched for her entire life. "Everyone who drinks this water will be thirsty again," He told her, "but whoever drinks the water I give him will never thirst" (John 4:13–14). Five husbands plus assorted lovers couldn't quench her thirst, but the good news Jesus told her did. She discovered the Messiah and plunged her life on Him. After that fateful meeting she too would say, "I shall not be in want. I know the Lord, so I have everything that I need."

When we know the Lord, we do not need or want anything else. Asaph wrote, "Earth has nothing I desire besides you" (Psalm 73:25). These words were more than church talk at a testimony service. Earlier in the psalm he wrote of looking at all the world had to offer. His heart felt a twinge of jealousy because of the prosperity of the wicked. He wondered what it would be like to have no struggles, to have everything the world has to offer. In the midst of his personal pity party, Asaph stopped and focused upon the Lord. The vision of God in His sanctuary made all that the world can grasp seem nothing more than a dream that evaporates with the morning light. As he focused upon the Lord he sang out, "God is the strength of my heart and my portion forever" (Psalm 73:26).

Paul found Asaph's words to be true. In comparison to knowing Christ, he wrote the church in Philippi, everything else is nothing but garbage. Unlike most of us, Paul lost all that he had for the sake of following Christ. But he wasn't alone. Throughout history we find men and women gladly surrendering everything the world holds dear, everything the world says they need, for the sake of knowing the Lord. The writer of the book of Hebrews describes those who have discovered this truth with these words:

> Others were tortured and refused to be released, so that they might gain a better resurrection. Some faced jeers and flogging, while still others were chained and put in prison. They were stoned; they were sawed in two; they were put to death by the sword. They went about in sheepskins and goatskins, *destitute, persecuted and mistreated* —the world was not worthy of them. They wandered in deserts and mountains, and in caves and holes in the ground. These were all commended for their faith, yet none of them received what had been promised. (Hebrews 11:35–39, italics added)

Destitute, persecuted, mistreated, yet they had everything they needed. That is the message of the second line of the Twenty-third Psalm. The Lord is all we need. Even if we have nothing else, even if we live the life David endured for many years, a life of fleeing from city to city, not knowing where our next meal will come from, not knowing if the person we trust will betray us; even if we lose everything for the sake of Christ, we have everything that we need, for we have the Lord.

When we have the Lord we have more than our minds can comprehend. Ephesians 1:3 assures us that the Lord has blessed us with every spiritual blessing in

Christ. He did not forget anything. *Every* spiritual bless-ing, everything we could possibly hope for, is ours in Christ. We don't have to wait for some distant time in the future when we finally walk through the gates of heaven to begin enjoying them. God started pouring His bless-ings on us long before we were born, long before the earth was even created.

Before the creation of the world, He chose us to be holy and blameless in His sight (Ephesians 1:4). After we came into this world, we wandered aimlessly, lost and hopeless. God changed all that by adopting us into His family. We were slaves of sin, but God redeemed us through the death of His Son. Our sins permanently sep-arated us from God; He swept them aside by giving us forgiveness. He has guaranteed all these blessings with the seal of His Holy Spirit whom He freely gives to those who believe in His Son. As if all of this were not enough, He promises to give us an eternal inheritance in His presence in heaven. What more could we ask for?

Yet He doesn't stop there. The first chapter of the book of Ephesians goes on to tell us that when we come to know Christ God gives us far more than we could ever imagine. He sets us free from fear and guilt and death. Because this world can be so cold and cruel, He fills our lives with joy. Without Him life meanders along aimlessly; with Him we find the true purpose for our existence. In times of grief He gives us comfort and hope, and in times of trials He assures us that everything we go through is a part of His plan for our lives. He guards us, guides us, and listens for the sound of our voice calling out in prayer. Everything He does, He does because He loves us with a love we can never understand. This love never fails. It remains as consistent as our God, who constantly draws us into an intimate relationship with Himself. With Him as our Shepherd, we have everything that we need.

But . . . the car still has too many miles on it and the refrigerator keeps making that noise and the waist seems to have shrunk on most of our good pants and the bank would like the mortgage payment on time this month. David tells us that the Lord is all we need, but the kids need new shoes and the dog needs her shots and then there is the gas bill and the electric bill and the phone bill and the water bill. We would rather think about love and joy and comfort and hope, because thinking about our bank balance and the bills in the mailbox makes us depressed. The Lord is my Shepherd, but the wolf is at the door.

Before our bleating reaches His ears, our Shepherd knows what we need. He has been watching us. He knows about the surprise phone call from the school nurse and the high cost of X-rays. We may not know how we can fit another repair bill into an overstretched budget, but He already has a plan. As the cost of living climbs along with our blood pressure, the Lord tells us,

> Do not worry about your life, what you will eat; or about your body, what you will wear. . . . For the pagan world runs after all such things, and your Father knows that you need them. But seek his kingdom, and these things will be given to you as well. (Luke 12:22, 30–31)

Don't worry; God knows what we need. Seek His kingdom, seek Him above all things, and He will take

41

care of the rest. The Lord is our Shepherd. We can trust Him. Shepherds in the ancient Near East put the welfare of the flock ahead of themselves. The Lord is no exception. He loves us and will care for us. Our part of the equation is to exercise faith, pursue the eternal rather than worrying about the temporal, and leave our needs in God's hands.

That is so easy to write, I think I'll do it again. Exercise faith, pursue the eternal, and leave everything else to God to worry about. Nothing to it . . . writing it, that is. Putting these words into practice is another matter entirely. Placing a doctor's bill we can see into the hand of the God we cannot see is a bit unnerving. The thought always races through our minds, *What if He doesn't come through? What if God does not provide?* It's not that we want to question His faithfulness, but what if He already provided the money we need but we mistakenly spent it on tickets to a ball game?

The Shepherd has already anticipated our unease. "Do not be afraid, little flock, for your Father has been pleased to give you the kingdom" (Luke 12:32). Relax. When the Lord is our Shepherd, we already have everything we need. He has given us an eternal inheritance reserved in heaven for us, so we do not need to worry about something as trivial as money. In fact, He goes on to tell us that instead of worrying about having enough, we need to start giving away what we have. "Sell your possessions and give to the poor" (Luke 12:33), Jesus told His disciples. Freedom from worry enables us to follow our Lord's example and give to those in need. Not only will we find that all of our needs have been taken care of, but we will also discover the joy of generosity and the freedom from anxiety it brings. Trust the Lord with your needs. He is faithful.

The Lord is my Shepherd; I shall not be in want. When I have Him, what more could I ask for? Unfortunately I do find myself asking for more. I don't mean to. I try to silence the cravings; I tell myself He will provide everything I need. My needs aren't the problem. My wants are. The psalmist said earth had nothing he desired besides the Lord. I believe that. I try to live it. But then I listen to the words coming out of my mouth. They reveal what is going on inside my heart. It's a revelation I could live without.

I still find myself walking through the maze of wants and desires that opened this chapter. My needs are pretty simple. All I really need is something to eat, a place to sleep, and clothes for my body. People in other parts of the globe content themselves with a steady diet of rice and beans for the first need. I read in the Bible of people who slept in tents their entire lives. Not too many generations ago most people had only one or two sets of clothes. But I don't want to subsist on rice and beans. I want enchiladas and Kung Pao chicken and spaghetti with loads of garlic. Tents are cold, and the ground is too hard. If I am away from my own mattress for more than a night or two, I get cranky from lack of sleep. (Anyway, if I sleep in a tent every night I'll be counted as "homeless" when the next census is taken.) And I cannot imagine getting by with one or two changes of clothes. I am like you—my closet is so full that I occasionally have to throw out old clothes to make room for the new.

The whole idea of choosing to be content with the

Lord alone is foreign to those of us in the Western world. But that is exactly what we must do. We must choose to agree with David and say, "With the Lord as my Shepherd, I don't need anything else." The second line of the Shepherd's song is a call to you and me to lay our desires at the feet of Christ. When the Lord is our Shepherd, we have everything that we need. As an old writer says, "he who has God and everything else has no more than he who has God only."[2] If this is true, we must begin to pursue God with an unquenchable passion. Enough time has been wasted on the trivial. He offers us everything we could possibly desire when He offers us Himself.

We come into this life making demands. There are a few things we think we need, but there is only one that we really do need. The Lord is my Shepherd. I shall not be in want when my heart is set on Him.

NOTES

1. Quoted in C. S. Lewis, *The Weight of Glory and Other Addresses* (New York: Macmillan, 1949), 2.
2. Ibid., 7.

Chapter Three

HE MAKES ME
LIE DOWN IN
GREEN PASTURES

He made me mow my green pastures. I didn't understand what He was doing at the time. From my perspective I saw it as the only job I could find. It wasn't my first time to make a career of walking behind a lawn mower, yet I never expected to be back mowing yards for just over minimum wage at the age of thirty-one. Not with a family to support. Not with a degree in theology. Not after seven years in the pastorate. Not after God moved my family and me more than two thousand miles. I never thought He moved us that far so I could mow yards all day every day.

David said the Lord made him lie down in green pastures. During my tenure in the pastureland, I wished I could be so lucky. Life wasn't turning out the way I expected. His plan didn't make any sense. From sunup to sundown I mowed and sweated and stank. My legs and arms were covered with poison ivy. The sight and smell of me made people move away when I walked into

McDonald's for lunch. I complained to God, even argued with Him, until He opened my eyes to see His grace. God wasn't punishing me. Far from it. He brought me to the green pastures to save my ministry.

As David described life as a sheep under the Great Shepherd, he began with a scene that was common in his time. In the ancient Near East, good pastureland was difficult to find throughout most of the year. The summer heat left the Judean hills brown and dry. In order to keep their sheep alive, shepherds kept the flock on the move in search of food. Their search often took them far from home, but they didn't have any choice. Sheep needed grass. Shepherds had to find it.

Once the rain began to fall the hills changed dramatically. Dusty brown gave way to brilliant green. David described this time of year in the third line of the Twenty-third Psalm, "He makes me lie down in green pastures." He painted a picture of mid-November, when the grass is just starting to flourish. The term he chose for green describes the tender, young grass that grows early in the rainy season. For a shepherd, the sight of this grass was a welcome relief. His work became much easier. His sheep's essential daily requirements could be found on the nearest hillside. A shepherd could stop trekking across the countryside and let the sheep, and himself, rest.

But sheep won't just lie down and stay there. If animals could develop ulcers, sheep would live on Zantac. The slightest provocation shifts their minds to panic mode. Tension within the flock and the irritating influence of flies and parasites keeps them restless and nervous. Stopping to rest isn't a sheep decision in the Twenty-third Psalm. The shepherd forces them down. He knows what is best for them. He knows they need to rest.

He makes us lie down to rest as well.

Throughout Scripture we find that God places a premium on rest. For six days He designed and created the world, then on the seventh day He rested. Long before Moses received the Ten Commandments on top of Mount Sinai, God blessed the seventh day of the week and set it aside as a Sabbath, a time of rest. In the law the Lord set aside regular times of national rest and renewal. Even the land was to rest. Every seven years Israel's farmers were to refrain from planting crops. Unwisely, they ignored this command. Therefore, God allowed the tribes of Israel to be carried off into exile by Babylon for seventy years so that the land might enjoy its Sabbaths (2 Chronicles 36:21).

You and I mean more to God than the fields of Canaan. He doesn't just command us to take a day off; He holds His rest out to us as a promise:

> There remains, then, a Sabbath-rest for the people of God; for anyone who enters God's rest also rests from his own work, just as God did from his. Let us, therefore, make every effort to enter that rest, so that no one will fall by following [Israel's] example of disobedience. (Hebrews 4:9–11)

Because of all that our Shepherd has done for us in Christ, we can rest from our efforts to earn our salvation. We can stop trying to win God's favor and rest in His grace offered to us through the Cross. As if this were not enough, He also promises to make this rest complete by bringing us into His presence forever and ever. On that day our struggle with sin and our flesh and all the problems of this world will give way to the unspeakable joy of the world to come as we sit at the feet of the Lord for all eternity.

As wonderful as that promise sounds, God never intended for us to wait until our lives are over to stop and rest in Him. We can enjoy His rest now. Jesus showed us the way. His Father gave Him three short years to fulfill all of the prophecies of the Old Testament and establish the kingdom of God on earth. With so much to do in so little time, Jesus should have been the ultimate workaholic. There were souls to save, sick people to heal, disciples to train. "I can't stop now, not with the eternal destiny of billions in the balance" would be the constant refrain of a normal human being. Reading the story of His life we expect to find Jesus frantically racing against the clock.

But when we retrace His steps we find that He was never in a hurry. He never ran from place to place, never developed an ulcer worrying about missing His next appointment. In fact, Matthew, Mark, Luke, and John describe a Man whose pace was deliberate, but never rushed. The weight of the task before Him never pulled His attention away from seeking His Father. He regularly found time to go up on a hill and do nothing but pray. While the crowds clamored for Him, He retreated to a quiet place to rest and find refreshment in His Father (Mark 1:35–37).

I find it ironic that those of us who claim to follow Christ fall so short of His example. We feel guilty when we slow down. Every day moves by a little faster than the day before. Early in the morning the alarm clock sounds and we hit the floor running. We rush around the house, scooting the kids out the door to school. Then it's off to work to build a career. Other cultures take naps at midday; we do power lunches. Five o'clock comes and we rush back home where the real fun begins. We run one child to piano lessons, another to gymnastics. On the way home we zip through the drive-through for dinner. Then it's off again to one daughter's basketball practice, where we sit and make calls on our cellular phone. But we can't stop yet, not with karate and PTA and church and some meeting whose purpose we can't remember waiting for us. At the end of the day we fall into bed, only to get up the next day and do it all over again.

I know this schedule by heart. I lived a variation of it for years. No one forced it on me. I gladly chose it for myself while I was in school training for the ministry. Never content to take my time, I loaded up my schedule and took classes during the summer terms in order to finish as fast as possible. My first staff position made school seem like a holiday. All five staff members in that rapidly growing church pushed and planned and drove the church, ever seeking to reach more people. Two years later I was the pastor of a small church in the hills of California, but I had big dreams. Five years later it had tripled in size, but I didn't have anything left to give. My spirit was dry, my mind exhausted. I hated the pastorate and was looking for some avenue of ministry that would allow me to fulfill my calling without serving in a church.

That is why I found myself in the middle of my pastoral career walking across the green pastures behind a lawn mower. For three months I did not preach or lead a Bible study or teach a Sunday school lesson. I did not do any of the things I had been trained to do. No one came to me for pastoral counseling, nor did a church look to me for vision and leadership. The Shepherd knew that all of the above had pushed me to my breaking point. My calling wasn't the problem. I was. I needed rest.

In the third line of the Twenty-third Psalm, David describes a wonderful gift of God's grace, a gift He extends to all of the sheep in His flock. There are times in our lives when our Lord throws the brakes on all of our plans and goals and dreams and schedules. He doesn't care what our organizers and calendars say, He knows what we need. He makes us lie down. At first we fight Him. Our small, sheep-ish minds cannot comprehend what is going on. All we can see are lost opportunities and wasted time. We keep jumping up, trying to run back to our routine, but the Shepherd stops us. He forces us down in the place we did not choose, the place we need to be, the green pastures. God in His grace keeps us there as long as it takes to calm our spirits and rest our souls.

He makes us lie down to relax.

Sheep on a Judean hillside would only lie down if the shepherd stayed in their sight. They knew if he was nearby they were safe. Finally they could relax. None of the sheep stood guard for the rest of the flock. The shepherd didn't need their help. If one well-meaning ram tried to inform the shepherd of all the dangerous beasts that could come running over the hill at any moment and devour the flock, the shepherd would simply calm its nerves and make it lie down with the rest of the sheep.

The flock didn't need to worry about tomorrow with the shepherd standing nearby. In the warm sunshine of the green pasture they could relax without a care in the world.

When God makes us rest, He also calls us to relax in Him. Human sheep struggle with the idea of relaxing. We can crash in front of the television and pass out during a ball game, but we have trouble surrendering all of the details of our lives to the Lord. There are problems to solve, decisions to make, dreams to chase. We need answers, and we need them now. Stepping back and giving someone else control over our lives is a scary proposition. Something deep within us screams out, demanding a role in the decision-making process.

In the midst of it all the Shepherd steps in. "Lie down," He says. "Are you worried about your life? Relax. Don't worry. I have everything under control. All you need to do is seek first My kingdom and My righteousness, and I will take care of the rest. Leave the details to Me" (see Matthew 6:25, 33). He can say this because He is the sovereign Lord of the universe. A sparrow cannot fall to the ground, nor can one of the hairs on our heads go down the shower drain, without Him noticing. If He can take care of all the sparrows on the planet, He can certainly handle the little things we find to worry about.

Like a shepherd calming down hyperactive sheep, the Lord makes us lie down to remind us of this fact. Lying at His feet we get a fresh new perspective on life, one that has Him squarely in control. Our anxiety doesn't make Him more aware of our lot in life. Worrying can't add a single hair to our heads (although it may have the opposite effect). Our great need is to learn to relax in the Lord by placing all of our needs and fears and frustrations in His hands. We can relax. He is Lord. He is the Shepherd.

He makes us lie down to enjoy His provision.

Living in a land where everything we could possibly need is as close as the nearest supermarket makes it hard to understand the concept of need. Not only does having so much keep us from appreciating need, it also causes us to take God's provision for granted. It is hard not to. A Filipino woman who had lived in the United States for less than a week understood the rest of us better than we understand ourselves. She commented at a church service after her first trip to Target, "Now I know why Americans pray so little. You don't need to pray: Everything you need is so close." We have so much, we often lose sight of God's hand in it all.

Western Christians may live with the delusion of self-sufficiency, but David never did. As he wrote the third line of the Twenty-third Psalm, he was in effect confessing his own dependence upon the Lord's provision and celebrating its sufficiency. God not only made him lie down, but He placed him in the best of all places. David's words describe every sheep's dream, a luscious green field of tender new grass. All of it is ours to enjoy, to eat our fill and roll around in. Celebrate! This isn't some somber line to be repeated in hushed tones. This is a sheep's dream come true. God is great! Wonderful! Better than we could ever imagine! "Taste and see that the Lord is good," David wrote in Psalm 34:8. He is greater and better than we ever imagined.

David celebrated all God gave him. I'm not sure if the same could be said of most of us. We thank Him, but the full weight of all He has done often slips by, unnoticed. Far too often you and I are guilty of limiting our vision to see only the material goods He has given us. When we step back and look at all He has promised us in His Word, we realize that words cannot describe the magnitude of it all. Everything we could want, everything we can imagine, everything that is eternal is ours in Christ. Paul told the church in Ephesus, "Praise be to the God and Father of our Lord Jesus Christ, who has blessed us in the heavenly realms with every spiritual blessing in Christ" (Ephesians 1:3).

When we fail to recognize how God's hand has provided all that we enjoy, the Lord will take the time to remind us. He will take away the toys we cling to and strip away all the peripheral items from our lives. He isn't being cruel. Instead He is opening the door to us to fall at His feet and worship Him. The language of Psalm 23:2 makes it clear that the sheep didn't just realize how great the Shepherd is one day while wandering around in the field. The Lord made them lie down. He opens our eyes to see all of life from His perspective. When He does, we are able to see that He has provided everything we could possibly need and more than we could ever hope to find.

He makes us lie down to listen.

While mowing my green pastures, I found that God has another reason for bringing our lives to a halt, a reason four-legged sheep cannot appreciate. As the pace of life accelerates, we never take the time to sit and be quiet before God. Noise blares at us from every room, people continually call our name (especially if we are mothers of one or more preschoolers), and everything is urgent. We run from one project to the next, one meeting to another, to ball practice, music lessons, recitals, church, and school, and before we even miss it, we lose the ability to hear the still, small voice of God.

Maybe it was during the commercials for new and improved dog food in the super-duper size bag, but somewhere along the line we bought the lie that bigger means better and busier means more effective. The more involved we are, the greater our responsibilities, the bigger the place we serve, the better we like it. I especially see this in myself and my fellow pastors. We justify our pursuit of bigger and better places of service and our mountain of activity by saying it all allows us to do more for God. But the very opposite is actually the case. Francis Schaeffer said it best in his essay, "No Little People, No Little Places": "If by taking a bigger place our quietness with God is lost, then to that extent our fellowship with Him is broken and we are living in the flesh, and the final result will not be as great, no matter how important the larger place may look in the eyes of other men or in our own eyes."

I believe we live in a time and place in history when being quiet before God is a lost art. Very few of us take the time to simply listen for His voice. If God wants to speak to us, He has to catch us. I must confess, I have broken off more than one session of prayer when I suddenly remembered some pressing phone call I needed to return or a deadline I must meet. We all have. The urgent finds a way to squeeze out the important, and few things are as important as listening to the voice of Almighty God. In the green pastures God filters out the useless noise in order that we might hear what our ears are straining for.

As I said at the beginning of the chapter, He used the back of a lawn mower as the place where my ears finally tuned Him in. He and I had some very interesting conversations during that summer in Louisville, Kentucky. At the beginning He allowed me to do all the talking. I moaned and cried and kept asking why. When I stopped talking long enough to listen, He answered. In a one-acre lot somewhere south of town, He finally slowed me down enough to get through to me. He started a conversation that lasted long after the grass died out and my days behind a mower ended. I heard Him renew my call into the ministry.

Every believer has the ability to hear God. Jesus said, "My sheep listen to my voice; I know them, and they follow me" (John 10:27). He said this as a statement of fact. Those who are part of His flock know the unique song of the Shepherd. Through His Word and the Holy Spirit who dwells within everyone who follows Christ, He communicates with us. God isn't silent. He speaks to every lamb in His flock.

He speaks, but do we listen? Do our ears labor to hear what He is saying? Do we spend time in His Word to discover what He will say to us today? Let's get real with ourselves and with God. He makes us lie down in the green pastures so that we can listen to His voice, know Him, and follow Him.

I shudder to think of where I would be today if He hadn't thrown me into the last job on earth I would have chosen. I was much too busy to really listen, even though I thought my ears were tuned in to Him. I was going here and there and doing so much but accomplishing nothing eternal. But the Shepherd loved me enough to cancel all my plans and make me lie down in the green pastures.

He made me mow my green pastures, and my life has never been the same.

Chapter Four

HE RESTORES

MY SOUL

*I*t's the traffic. Yeah, that's what does it. The traffic. Twice a day, every day, it's the same thing. Bumper-to-bumper, cars weaving in and out, missed exits, wasted time. Yuck. Who needs it?

Maybe it's the job. Yeah, that's what does it. The job. Today is exactly like yesterday, and tomorrow will be more of the same. The monotony, the predictability. Four years of college for this. Other jobs are out there, but the pay scale here would be hard to beat, although there are times when a change of scenery would be worth it.

It could be the children. Yeah, that's what does it. The children. It's not a question of love; it's a question of sanity. From early in the morning to late at night the house is a giant whirlwind of activity. "Mom this" and "Dad that" mixed in with a resounding chorus of "I need, I need, I need." Sure, kids are a blessing from the Lord, but even Mike and Carol Brady needed a break once in a while.

It has to be the church. Yeah, that's what does it. The

church. The sermons could be used for anesthesia. And the worship service. The songs haven't changed in fifty years. And the people. Some of them can drive a person insane. They complain about the most trivial things. No one is committed anymore. It's a wonder the doors stay open.

I think it's just life. I'm certain that's it. Life. Camping out on planet Earth will tire out the hardiest of souls. God said the world was very good on the day He created it, but things must have changed a lot since then. Everything in this world seems to be designed to wear us down. With bills to pay and responsibilities to fulfill and deadlines to meet, we all reach the place where we cannot go on any further. We're more than fatigued. Our souls have withered and dried up. Blame the traffic or the job or the kids or the church or fill in the blank, the end result is the same. We need to be revived.

David could have made quite a list of all the things that dried up his soul. Wearing the crown over God's chosen people was no easy task. He was responsible for everything that went on in the nation of Israel. People looked to him for answers to the unanswerable questions. The spiritual health of the nation was also his responsibility. David would either be the shining example or the ultimate excuse for everyone else's walk with God. On top of it all was the protection of the people themselves. The tiny land bridge that was Israel was surrounded by hostile nations, all intent on pushing Jacob's descendants into the sea. Every spring they tried to do just that. Unfortunately, David's enemies were not confined to the pagan nations. Rivals to the throne arose within the borders of Israel itself, even within his own family.

The weight of the crown took its toll on David. He too cried out for relief:

> I am poured out like water,
>   and all of my bones are out of joint.
> My heart has turned to wax;
>   it has melted away within me.
> My strength is dried up like a potsherd,
>   and my tongue sticks to the roof of my mouth;
> You lay me in the dust of death. (Psalm 22:14–15)

We all have times that we can relate to David's words. Tired. Weak. Dry. All we want to do is lie down and never get up.

When we reach this point, few verses speak to us like the fourth line of the Twenty-third Psalm: "He leads me beside quiet waters, he restores my soul." Just hearing the words is enough to make the tightness in my shoulders loosen up. David's words are more than a line of poetry; they give a promise all of us need to take advantage of. The Lord, the Great Shepherd, promises to lift us out of the dull, dry deadness of life and restore our soul. He will set us beside the quiet waters of life and let us drink our fill.

Take me now, Lord, I am ready. I am ready to kick back and relax, to feel some relief from life's worries and cares. Quiet waters, that sounds great. Maybe You could arrange to park a ski boat at the dock for a little R and R. Are there any fish in these waters? I hope so. Nothing recharges my batteries like hooking a lunker big-mouth bass. Ahhhh, just thinking about it makes me feel better. I could use a vacation. So could my wife and kids. Life wears down the heartiest of souls. There's nothing like a week or two out beside the still waters of the lake at a vacation resort to make a soul feel fresh, restored.

As we found in the last chapter, God does give us time of rest, but rest is not synonymous with His promise to restore our souls. The Hebrew term David used in the phrase "he restores my soul" paints a unique word picture. The word literally means to cause something to turn. In other Old Testament passages the word is translated *convert* or *repent*. The central idea of the word is a complete turnaround. David is in effect telling us that the Lord restores our souls by causing us to turn back to Him. The Shepherd does more than give our souls an energy boost. He sets us back into a right relationship with Himself by turning our eyes away from the world and setting them on Him alone. A restored soul is a soul in fellowship with the One who created us.

This is what we really need, not another vacation. God designed us in such a way that we need to be in constant fellowship with Him. As John 1:4 declares, in Him is life. We cannot live apart from Him. Jesus Himself said, "I am the vine; you are the branches. If a man remains in me and I in him, he will bear much fruit; apart from me you can do nothing" (John 15:5). Just as a branch needs the vine, we must stay in fellowship with the Lord to truly live. Once a branch is cut off from the vine it will shrivel up and die. It may stay green for a few days, but the end result will always be the same. The life of a branch comes from the vine. Real life flows into us from the Lord.

But a flood of distractions tries to pull us away from Him. Let's be honest; it's difficult trying to stay connected to an invisible God in a very visible world. It's hard to hear His inaudible voice with all the noise that echoes around us. We know He is nearby, but it often feels like He is far away. Everywhere we look we see evidence of His handiwork, but we usually don't take the time to notice. If He would speak from heaven like He did when His Son was baptized, that would keep our attention. But He doesn't, and we get distracted. With our hearts we tell Him we love Him, yet our minds are so filled with clutter that we can go days, sometimes weeks, without giving Him a thought, even though He is our one true source of life. God designed us to live in close fellowship with Him, yet the world keeps pulling us away.

There are a lot of things we can blame, all of them valid: our jobs, family responsibilities, money, boredom, and a host of others. When we refuse to obey the Lord or fall into outright sin, we separate ourselves from Him. Other times we place something as insignificant as a professional football team before the Lord and find ourselves shriveling spiritually. But we usually cannot put the finger of blame on any one thing, any one act of sin. We simply drift away. Our spiritual passion reaches an all-time low, and our focus shifts away from the Lord.

A few years ago I found myself in that very predicament. It happened so slowly, so subtly, that I did not realize what was happening until it was too late. I wrote the following to the Lord as He began to turn my soul back to Him:

> Distracted.
> How did I get so distracted?
> The path I find myself on is not the path I

intended to take. It seems that it just happened. I did not notice the direction I was going until it was too late. I was distracted while the path suddenly changed.

It is not as though I sought to rebel against God or to question Christ's lordship in my life. I diligently sought His direction day by day. I strained to see His footsteps before me in order that I might retrace His steps like a child following his father through the forest. But like a child chasing a butterfly, I looked away. My curiosity was tweaked. My eyes were turned. I became distracted.

Now I find myself in a place I never thought I would be. It is a place I visited before and swore I would never return. My theology was solid. Prayer and praise were constantly upon my lips. But the words ring hollow today, for I know where I am. I have left my first love. My heart has grown cold even as my mind grew full. Immersed in the things of God I find myself facing a long journey home. It is the path the prodigal walked so many years ago. As he hoped for the grace of the father I find that I too have only one hope, God's wonderful grace.

What will I say when I return? *Oh Lord, I didn't mean to go. It wasn't as if I sought to drift away from You. I was . . . distracted. Only for a moment. But the moment has lasted much too long.*

As I journey down the path home, I think about what it was that caught my eye. It seemed so small at the time. It was not one of the forbiddens. There are no commandments prohibiting it. Yet the longer it held my fancy the less room there was in my heart for single-minded devotion to God. Now this distraction doesn't seem so fascinating. It has become disgusting, as did the idols of old that pulled the people of Israel away from their first love.

I am going home. My foolish pride that refused to admit that I had lost my way has been taken away by the mire of the pit. Oh Lord, keep my eyes on You. The distractions are too costly. Keep me close to Your side.

When we become separated from the Lord is not the only time we need to have our souls restored. The world not only wears us down; it also wears us out. Many of David's psalms cry out for relief from godless men. The constant pursuit of his enemies and their assaults on his character drained David of all his strength. We hear him cry out in Psalm 6, "I am worn out from groaning, all night long I flood my bed with weeping and drench my couch with tears. My eyes grow weak with sorrow; they fail because of all my foes." David hadn't forsaken the Lord, but he felt like the Lord may have forsaken him. When the cruelty of life overwhelms us, we can relate to David. We need what he found in the Twenty-third Psalm.

The Lord promises that whatever the cause, He will turn our souls back to Him. This is not some sort of mystical mind game. It is very, very real. David spoke of this restoration coming at a specific place, beside the quiet waters. Obviously, sheep need water to survive. Yet I believe David had more than sheep in mind as he wrote these words.

Before he became king, David lived as a fugitive from King Saul. Enraged by jealousy, Saul led the armies of Israel in repeated manhunts, trying to kill the future king. David hid anywhere and everywhere, even going so far as to seek refuge among Israel's archenemies, the Philistines. Yet David's favorite place to hide, the place where both his physical and spiritual strength were restored, was the strongholds of En Gedi. Located near the Dead Sea in the midst of the Judean desert, En Gedi is an oasis of spring-fed waterfalls and pools, a place no one would ever expect to find in such a hot, dry region. This is the sort of place David must have had in mind when he wrote of the quiet waters—literally, waters of rest. The springs of En Gedi offered the perfect place to get alone with God, restoring the soul. The Lord continually uses places like En Gedi to take His children in order that He might restore their souls.

Elijah also found himself on the run from an angry king. The great prophet who prevailed in his showdown with the prophets of Baal on top of Mount Carmel had to flee for his life because of his actions there. The physical and emotional strain of his flight took its toll. When he could run no farther he sat under a broom tree and prayed, "I have had enough, Lord.…Take my life; I am no better than my ancestors" (1 Kings 19:4). Elijah didn't know it, but God wasn't finished with him. He asked to die, but the Lord intended to take him directly to heaven without Elijah having to go through the pain of death. But before Elijah could finish the work God had planned for him in the meantime, he needed to be restored. His eyes were so focused upon evil King Ahab and his wife Jezebel that he forgot who the true King of kings and Lord of lords was.

God took Elijah to a special place, a mountaintop. It

was the same mountain upon which the Lord gave the law to Moses. Alone together on Mount Horeb, the Lord spoke to Elijah in a gentle whisper. The prophet came down from the mountain with a renewed resolve and a refreshed spirit.

The Lord used a place to restore Elijah for the same reason He takes us to isolated getaways. If we stay in our normal routine, with our overbooked schedules and constant interruptions, we have trouble hearing His voice. He would have to use thunder and lightning and all sorts of pyrotechnics to get through to us. But when He gets us alone in a quiet place He is able to get our full and undivided attention. Then and only then is He able to turn our souls back to Him. This special place does not have to be beside the waters of En Gedi or on a mountaintop half a world away. Jesus told us to pray daily in such a place: "When you pray, go into your room, close the door and pray to your Father" (Matthew 6:6). The quiet place of restoration can be as close as a secluded room in your house.

The Lord also restores our souls through people. Two men played such a role in the life of David. One encouraged him when he was tired and defeated; the other rebuked him when he fell into sin. Both were used by God to turn David's eyes and heart back to the Lord. The first man, Jonathan, was closer than a brother to David. The two should have been rivals. David was God's choice as the next king of Israel; Jonathan, the oldest son of King Saul, was the natural heir. Rather than compete with each other, their hearts were joined together as one. At one point in his life as a fugitive, David was worn down. Even the people of Israel for whose homes David had fought were against him. When David was beaten down and ready to give up, Jonathan came to him and "helped him find strength in God" (1 Samuel 23:16).

The other man God used to turn David's heart back to the Lord went to him at a very different time in his life. Many years after he became king of Israel David committed an act that threatened to destroy himself and the kingdom. In the spring of the year when he should have been off to war, David looked down from his roof and saw another man's wife. He sent for her, slept with her, and tried to cover his sin by having her husband killed in battle. If anyone knew what David did, they did not have the courage to confront him. That is, none did except for one man. Nathan the prophet went to David and confronted him with his sin. Because of Nathan's words, David repented. Nathan turned the king back to God.

Jonathan and Nathan both illustrate the way in which God uses individuals to turn our hearts back to Him. For this reason it is absolutely critical that we pursue meaningful relationships with brothers and sisters in Christ. We need one another. None of us have the intestinal fortitude to survive in this life on our own. The spiritual battles we face are far more than we can ever win on our own. We need other people to stand beside us and keep us going when we would rather give up. Most of us have a natural tendency to overlook our own weaknesses. We need other people who can hold us accountable and keep our eyes on the Lord.

God also employs a variety of other tools to bring the promise of restoration down to earth and into our lives. He works through music, books, sermons, Sunday school lessons, even conversations in an ice-cream store. Yet there is always one common denominator: It is the Lord who takes the initiative and turns our hearts back to Him. He pulls us back through His Spirit, He rearranges the course of our lives by His providence, and He speaks through His people. Always it is God who acts first. We turn back to Him in response to His actions.

I don't know why He does this. As I wrote these words, all sorts of memories flooded my mind, memories of times God brought the flow of my life to a screeching halt in order that He might bring me back to His side. There are so many places He has used: the youth camp in Oklahoma, the cabin in the Sierras, the mountains of New Mexico; so many people; so many times, when God intervened. He pulled me back even when I didn't know I had gone astray. He restored my soul. And He can restore yours.

Chapter Five

HE GUIDES ME

IN PATHS OF

RIGHTEOUSNESS

*O*ur natural human understanding of the nature of life is completely wrong. From the time a baby first becomes aware of the world around him, he assumes that everything revolves around him. In his eyes he is the most important person in the world. A few years in the real world makes each of us understand that we are only tiny blips on the radar screen of humanity. Nearly six billion people inhabit this planet that is nothing more than a speck in the universe. But when we get up in the morning and look in the mirror, our natural inclination is to assume that the person looking back at us is the apex of human history.

That is, until we open the Bible and listen to the message that flows from every page. From beginning to end Scripture declares that this life, this world, this everything is not about you or me. It is all about God. Every book from Genesis to Revelation declares His majesty and glory. All that is, was, and ever will be was created by

Him and for Him. The beauty He placed in nature came out of His good pleasure. He decided that the grass would be green and the sky would be blue. The incredible variety of plants and animals, some of which cannot be seen by the human eye, was all designed by Him. With the touch of a master artist, He splashed beauty and color across creation simply because He wanted to.

He decided to save you and me for the same reason. Listen to the way Paul summarized this thought in the first chapter of the book of Ephesians:

> In love he predestined us to be adopted as his sons through Jesus Christ, in accordance with his pleasure and will—to the praise of his glorious grace, which he has freely given us in the One he loves. . . . And he made known to us the mystery of his will according to his good pleasure. (Ephesians 1:5, 9)

God chose to love us and bring us into His family because it pleased Him. He decided to let us in on the eternal mystery of His will because doing so brought Him joy. The eternal, sovereign Lord was not moved to create us or save us because He lacked something. Rather, He brought us into this world and into His family out of the depths of His glorious grace.

We exist for God; He does not exist for us. He has placed His name upon those He saves in order that we might bring glory to His name. The mighty Lord of the universe doesn't exist in order that He might save a failing marriage or help us cope with a stressful day. Our calling is to surrender our lives to Him, not to find a way to use God to get what we want out of life. God is the meaning of life; He is more than a way for us to make sense out of the modern world. All of creation, both the visible and the invisible, things on earth and things in heaven, everything that is, was, and ever will be revolves around Him. God is the all in all.

David understood how this truth changes the way we live when he wrote the words, "He guides me in paths of righteousness *for his name's sake*" (Psalm 23:3b, italics added). The final four words reveal one of God's primary purposes in assuming the task of shepherding our lives. He cares for us and leads us for the sake of His name. Personal names carried a great deal of importance in Old Testament times. Parents selected names as a way of placing a blessing on a child. A person's character was conveyed by a name. This was especially true of the name of God. When Moses wondered who spoke to him through the burning bush, the Lord revealed Himself by His name, *I AM who I AM*. His name is so significant that the third commandment forbade its misuse. When Israel later turned from God to all sorts of idols, the Lord rebuked them, for they had profaned His name among the nations. The name of the Lord carries with it His reputation, for His name and His person are indistinguishable from one another. Through His name the Lord reveals His holiness and majesty.

When David spoke of God leading us *for His name's sake,* he was telling us why God would stoop so low as to get involved in the daily affairs of people like you and me. Through His people the Lord reveals Himself to the world. Like the people of Israel before us, God has placed His name on those who follow His Son by faith. We are Christians, Christlike, the people of God, God's elect, God's temple, His workmanship. Much more than our own reputations is on the line when we interact with the people of the world. The way we live our lives, the way we react to stressful situations, the choices we make when tempted, everything we say and do—all of it reveals God to the world. What people believe about the Lord depends on what they see in those of us who bear His name.

The crucial issue in our lives is always the reputation of the Lord. He guides us into paths of righteousness in order that He might reveal Himself to the world through us. The prophet Ezekiel reminded the Jews that the law was given for this same purpose:

> But for the sake of my name I did what would keep it from being profaned in the eyes of the nations. . . . I led them out of Egypt. . . . I gave them my decrees and made known to them my laws. . . . Also I gave them my Sabbaths as a sign between us, so they would know that I the Lord made them holy. (Ezekiel 20:9a, 10a, 11a, 12)

By observing the law the Jews proclaimed that there was only one God, the Lord, and He is holy. The law isn't the only place we find this truth. Jesus repeated its essence in the Sermon on the Mount when He said, "In the same way, let your light shine before men, that they may see your good deeds and praise your Father in heaven" (Matthew 5:16).

It is not just our performance that magnifies the name of the Lord in the eyes of the world. If it were we would be in trouble. All of us struggle with sin. Even David, the man who wrote the Twenty-third Psalm, committed horrible acts and brought disgrace on God's name. If God's reputation in the world depends on how we live our lives, we have a serious problem. Jeremiah could speak for all of us when he cried out to the Lord, "Although our sins testify against us, O Lord, do something for the sake of your name" (Jeremiah 14:7).

He has done something. For His name's sake He sent His Son to redeem us from sin. The forgiveness we often take for granted came at a great personal cost to God. Christ died to save us, yet the end result is that "at the name of Jesus every knee should bow, in heaven and on earth and under the earth, and every tongue confess that Jesus Christ is Lord, to the glory of God the Father" (Philippians 2:10–11). When the Lord saves us, His love and unlimited patience are put on display for the world to see. As a result, He is given praise, honor, and glory. He showers us with mercy and clothes us in the righteousness of Christ, a righteousness we could never achieve through our own efforts, all for the sake of His name.

Righteousness is not just a decree God makes concerning the redeemed but a way of life for those who follow Him by faith. David said, "He guides me *in paths of righteousness* for his name's sake." His choice of words paints a vivid picture. The word "path" refers to a trail that is well worn from being heavily traveled. The ancient Israelites did not pave their roads. Paths such as those between farmer's fields were maintained through constant traffic. The Hebrew term translated "righteousness" refers to a moral standard that is found in the nature and will of God. Taken together, Psalm 23:3 calls us to continually walk in the example of God's character.

To practice righteousness means to put the character of God revealed to us in His Word into action through our lives. Psalm 119:32 declares, "I run in the path of your commands, for you have set my heart free." Verse 105 of the same psalm calls God's Word a "lamp to my feet and a light for my path." All of the commands in the Bible flow from the Lord's character. When we walk in His law, we imitate God Himself. The law condemns sin in every form because sin is the very opposite of the Holy One. If we are to be holy as He is holy, we must guard against every sort of transgression.

But there is much more to the law and righteousness than avoiding sin. All of the "thou shalt nots" in the Old Testament are balanced by positive commands that should characterize the people of God. The third commandment tells us not to misuse the name of the Lord our God; Deuteronomy 6:5 tells us to love the Lord our God with all our heart and with all our soul and with all our strength. The eighth commandment says, "Do not steal"; Deuteronomy 15:10 calls us to give generously to those in need. The tenth commandment tells us not to covet any of our neighbors' possessions; Leviticus 19:18 commands us to love our neighbor as ourselves.

The life of Job gives us a perfect picture of what real righteousness looks like. He was so meticulous in his walk with the Lord that God Himself declared, "There is no one on earth like him; he is blameless and upright, a man who fears God and shuns evil" (Job 1:8). Not only did he offer sacrifices and pray, but this righteous man also imitated God by rescuing the poor when they cried for help and by caring for the fatherless (Job 29:12). He cared for widows and defended the cause of victims of injustice (vv. 13, 17). People saw in Job a man who was eyes to the blind, feet to the lame, a father to the needy, a man who took up the case of the stranger (vv. 15–16).

Job never had access to the Ten Commandments or the Word of God. He was born long before the first page of Scripture was written, yet his standards of righteousness put most of us to shame. He imitated the character of God, even though he never had a Bible to read. The Lord led Job in paths of righteousness just as He led David, just as He leads you and me. He calls us to do more than abstain from abusing alcohol and drugs. He longs to make us more than a people who are against sin. To walk in paths of righteousness means to invade our world with the holiness and passion that flows from our Lord.

We don't have to think long or hard to discover how to do this. Moses tells us to show hospitality to strangers (Deuteronomy 10:18), show respect for the elderly (Leviticus 19:32), and give to the poor (Deuteronomy 15:7–11). The prophets call us to defend the oppressed (Amos 5:11, 23–24), show mercy and compassion (Zechariah 7:9), and honor the marriage covenant (Malachi 2:14). Jesus told us to love our enemies and do good to those who mistreat us (Luke 6:27–29). He commands us to feed the hungry, clothe the poor, and visit those in hospitals and prison (Matthew 25:31–46). As if that weren't enough, He calls us to sell our possessions and give to the poor (Luke 12:33).

True holiness means more than kicking a bad habit. To walk in paths of righteousness means living a life that puts all of the above into practice on a daily basis. Let's be honest—this isn't exactly what we bargained for. Christianity has become a very private pursuit in our age. We look to Christ to help us feel better about ourselves, but we aren't so sure we want to spend our lives helping the sort of down-and-outers He spent most of his time with. Besides, we're busy. Very busy. Who has time to get involved? Isn't it enough that we stopped using foul language and cut back on watching television? We go to church, we try to do what Jesus would do, but what more is there?

When we follow the Lord down paths of righteousness, we find that there is a lot more. The paths He guides us down always intersect with people and situations who need a fresh touch of the Almighty. Psalm 23 reminds us of how much God loves us. As we follow Him, He wants to put us in places where other people can feel His love through us. The biblical definition of righteousness involves placing those who bear the name of the Lord in contact with those who need to know Him. It is a total way of life where we care for those who are in distress while keeping ourselves unstained by the world (James 1:27). Most of us think that if we do the latter, that is enough. It's not. Obedience to God's Word means obeying all of it, even the parts that inconvenience us and get our hands dirty.

And God will make sure we come to places where we need to roll up our sleeves and put righteousness into action. David reminds us that *"He guides [us] in paths of righteousness for his name's sake."* I love the picture David draws. He could have chosen one of several others. David well could have said, "He drives us." Imagine the Almighty on a horse with a whip pushing us up the trail like in an Old West cattle drive. None of us would dare slow down for fear of the lash. But the Lord doesn't drive us, in spite of what some of us think.

Or David could have said, "He tricks us onto paths of righteousness." The Lord could use the old bait-and-switch scam. All the promises of heaven and forgiveness and joy would be nothing more than a carrot to trick us into doing what we really don't want to do.

Or maybe he should have said that the Lord pays us to walk down paths of righteousness. Obeying His commandments are the price you have to pay to earn admission into heaven. If you don't make it far enough down the path, you're out of luck. The Lord is always watching, always keeping score. Only the top 10 percent get in, so you had better get to work.

If a frustrated parent rather than a shepherd had written the psalm, he would have said, "He drags us down paths of righteousness." Somewhere in the next few verses would be something like "This is for your own good, young man," or maybe "This will hurt me a lot more than it hurts you." A parent also might have written, "He begs us to go down paths of righteousness."

Sometimes we forget that the Lord doesn't use any of the above methods to move us to where we need to go, even though we assume He does. Our Shepherd *guides* us in paths of righteousness. The Hebrew term David used speaks of the way God governs men. He leads us along the path; all we need to do is follow.

Out of His love and grace the Shepherd makes following Him easy. He clearly lays out the path for us. The term for path describes a well-worn trail, easy to see, easy to follow. When we follow Him in paths of righteousness, He doesn't take us into uncharted territory. Innumerable multitudes have walked this path before us. Their tracks remain visible today. And the Lord makes sure we don't get sidetracked by walking in front of us. The Hebrew word translated "guide" is also used in Exodus 13:21 to describe the pillar of fire leading the children of Israel through the wilderness on their way to the Promised Land. By day the pillar took the form of a cloud that stood in sharp contrast to the desert sky. At night the cloud came alive with fire. Every person who made the trip with Moses from Egypt to Canaan could see the cloud by day and the fire at night. No one needed to stop and ask for directions. All they had to do was look up; God led the way.

Just as He led Israel thousands of years ago, the Shepherd leads us today. Sometimes we wish we could see a physical manifestation of His presence, but He has given us something even more remarkable. God places His Spirit inside everyone who receives His Son as Savior. Ezekiel saw this promise long before it became a reality when he wrote, "And I will put my Spirit in you and move you to follow my decrees and be careful to keep my laws" (Ezekiel 36:27). The Holy Spirit within us works with the Bible to clearly show us the path He has for us to travel. He plants the desire to follow within us and reminds us of what we should do at just the right time.

The Lord also made the path clear through the example He set when Jesus walked on this earth. At the time of this writing, the fashionable thing to wear is a little fabric bracelet with the letters WWJD, which stand for "What would Jesus do?" We don't have to guess as to what He would do in most situations. His example is very clear. What should we do when we face temptation? Jesus has already shown us the way by defeating

Satan with the Word of God. What should we do when we face opposition? The Pharisees opposed Jesus at every turn, but He never stooped to their level. He stayed faithful to the Father, unmoved in His commitment to do His will. What should we do when doing the will of God becomes excruciatingly difficult? In the Garden of Gethsemane, Jesus wrestled with the same question, yet He walked out of the garden declaring, "May Your will be done."

There are times when the path the Lord blazes for us seems fuzzy. We don't have a clue as to what Jesus would do, and sometimes we don't even care. Yet in those moments, God continues to guide us. Long ago He promised to never leave us or forsake us. No matter what we may go through, He will always guide us. He will always be there to take us by the hand and lead us to the place He wants us to be. We don't have to be aware of what He is doing. After all, He's the one in charge. He guides us in paths of righteousness for His name's sake.

Chapter Six

THOUGH I WALK
THROUGH THE VALLEY
OF THE SHADOW. . . .

$\mathcal{I}$t doesn't feel like a religious experience. Nor does it seem particularly spiritual, moving, or life-changing. Nothing about it seems like the stuff of testimony services, at least not while the valley walls still surround you. The words "nightmare" and "living hell" come closer to describing it. Your thoughts don't naturally run to how close the Lord seems. You pray constantly, but the words don't sound like anything you've ever uttered before. All you want to do is escape, to move out of the shadows of the valley.

Every turn along the valley floor holds another unwanted surprise. There is much to fear there, lurking in the darkness, waiting. A few souls march in with their heads held high in defiance. The sound of their voices echoes through the canyon, calling, "I will not be afraid." Before long they join the rest of us, nervously creeping along the middle path, quickly turning at every noise. The valley of the shadow delights in pushing human courage and confidence to the edge, then shoving them over it.

The valley is filled with shadows. Like the ninth plague on Egypt, it is a darkness that can be felt. Nothing can pierce it. What light there is refuses to divulge anything beyond one or two steps. Yet you cannot stand still. The cold makes you move forward. The cold and the voices. The sound of the voices is almost deafening. They don't come from the valley floor. Most of the travelers can hardly muster more than a hoarse whisper. The loudest voices come from above, from those watching as you stumble along. Although they intend to be voices of encouragement, most are little more than an annoying noise, a noise you would rather live without.

Job felt the icy darkness. He knew the pain of the wounds the valley inflicts. And he heard the voices, three of them, filling his ears with unwanted (and useless) advice. The Bible gives us surprisingly few details of Job's life. One thing we know about him: he lived in the valley of the shadow of death. The phrase occurs more times in the book that bears his name than in the rest of the Old Testament books combined. It is a hard book to read. We expect to see a hero boldly standing against Satan's harshest attacks. Listening to his words, he doesn't sound very bold. Or spiritual. "I wish I had died before any eye saw me. If only I had never come into being, or had been carried straight from the womb to the grave!" he cried out (Job 10:18–19). His words don't make any sense, except to people in the valley of the shadow. He says what everyone else is thinking.

David was no stranger to the valley of the shadow, yet he doesn't sound at all like Job. His words have the air of someone the darkness could not shake. "Even though I walk through the valley of the shadow of death, I will fear no evil, for you are with me" (Psalm 23:4). If anyone else had penned these words we would immediately dismiss them as the musings of someone whose feet had never hit the valley floor. But David's life was marked by darkness and tragedy. He endured the deaths of three children along with the senseless killing of his best friend. Many times his own life was in danger. Even after he became king he once had to flee Jerusalem to save his own skin. The same man who wrote "I will fear no evil" also wrote "I am worn out from groaning; all night long I flood my bed with weeping and drench my couch with tears" (Psalm 6:6). He knew the valley of the shadow of death, and the truth he discovered there gives the rest of us strength to press on to the other side.

The Hebrew term translated "the shadow of death" in Psalm 23:4 is used eighteen times in the Old Testament. The word is used to describe a place of darkness and gloom. Job uses it to describe a "land of deepest night, of deep shadow and disorder, where even the light is like darkness" (Job 10:22), like the pitch-black at the bottom of a mine shaft (Job 28:3–4). The prophets use the term to draw a picture of a land of darkness, whose inhabitants stumble helplessly as if they are blind with no one to lead them (Isaiah 9:1; Jeremiah 13:16). The term appears four times in the book of Psalms. Each time it describes the deep darkness that feels like God has abandoned His people (Psalm 44:19; 107:10, 14). Every time the word is used it conjures up the same sense of despair and hopelessness. The valley of the shadow of death is a place no one wants to walk.

Unfortunately, many of us will find ourselves in its icy grip at some point in our lives. I am not talking about facing trials. The valley of the shadow of death goes far beyond any ordinary test of our faith. It is a place where the very foundations of our lives are shaken. Everything we've ever counted on, everything we ever assumed to be true about God and His world, is rocked. The pain we experience in this place is too severe for words. It pierces the soul and makes us despair of life itself.

I always thought I had a pretty good grip on what David was talking about in Psalm 23:4. When I first took on this project, I knew how I would approach this phrase. I planned to paint a picture of the deep, intimate fellowship trials bring to those who endure them. Cheer up, I wanted to say, the valley may seem dark and deep, but the Lord is faithful, His fellowship sweet. Everything you are going through is worth it in light of the joy God will bring to you. Weeping may remain for a night, but rejoicing comes in the morning (Psalm 30:5). Don't despair; you will be rejoicing soon. I even planned to run to the book of Acts so we could all hear Paul and Silas singing in prison. If they sang in the darkness of a Roman dungeon, the Lord can put a song on all of our lips no matter what we may be going through.

All that sounded great, until the phone rang one December morning. It was one of those phone calls we all dread. Over the course of the next several months the Lord taught me more about the valley of the shadow of death than I ever wanted to know. In light of what He has shown me, I realize that I have never really been in the depths of the valley, at least not for very long. Even after the call I stood on one of the mountain passes, watching as people I loved suffered below. I do not now claim to be some expert on this matter. Quite the contrary. I understand how easily I overlooked an unpleasant place for fear that if I drew too close I might be sucked in.

This unpleasant place is closer than we might think. It appears over and over in the pages of Scripture. The best way to understand this place is to take a long look at it. No event better illustrates the horror of the valley than a period of David's life that began shortly after his sin with Bathsheba. I recommend you take the time to read about this in 2 Samuel 12:1 through 19:8. During a span of perhaps as many as ten years, David endured the death of an infant son, the rape of a daughter by her brother, a murder in the royal household, treason against him by a son he loved, and ultimately the death of that child. At one point he had to flee for his life while his subjects eagerly rejected him and embraced the one who plotted against him.

The writer of the book of Second Samuel placed all of these events together to show they were one long, painful trial for David. Several things stand out about his experience. First, the valley struck quickly and lasted far longer than he ever thought possible. Years dragged by without offering any relief. The journey through the valley of the shadow of death is always long and tiresome. Time stands still, so that even a few weeks seem like a lifetime. The length of the journey makes us wonder if we will ever get to the other side. The voices from overhead remind us that Psalm 23:4 says, "Even though I walk through the valley," as if the trip will be short. Yet the force of the original language emphasizes the time spent traveling in the midst of the valley of the shadow of death. It doesn't say a word about passing through to a destination on the other side.[1]

David also experienced the deep loneliness the valley stirs up within us. The darkness makes us assume that we are all alone. We know other people are nearby, and we know they are praying for us, but we still feel cut off from them. When we walk through life shaking with pain and sorrow, it is hard to imagine that anyone can fully understand the grief we feel. It is as though no one gets it, no one appreciates the seriousness of the situation. If they did they wouldn't say much of what they say. If they understood they wouldn't come to the hospital waiting room and immediately begin telling stories of what happened to Aunt Bertha when she had the same sort of surgery. In the valley you don't really care about what happened to Aunt Bertha; you long for some assurance that the light will shine again.

Listening to David's words, we find that the valley is a place where our confidence in ourselves is stripped away. It is a land of second-guessing, a land of questions. David's son Absalom conspired against him and stole his throne. His rebellion swept across the nation of Israel and ultimately led to a brief civil war. The rebellion ceased only after Absalom was struck down by Joab, the chief of David's armies. After squashing the rebellion, Joab's troops returned to the king with great joy, only to hear David lament, "O my son Absalom! My son, my son Absalom! If only I had died instead of you" (2 Samuel 18:33).

The pitch-black of the valley confuses our thinking. It leaves us constantly second-guessing our decisions. It also leaves us second-guessing God. "My God, my God, why have you forsaken me? Why are you so far from saving me, so far from the words of my groaning?" the Twenty-second Psalm asks. The words are a familiar refrain in the valley of the shadow of death. *Why are You so far away? Why?*

Yet David knew the Lord was nearby, for His hand was clearly visible in everything David went through. His trials came on him through an act of God, as a direct result of the Lord's discipline for David's great sin. This does not mean that every time you or I go through the darkness that God is displeased with us or paying us back for the wrong we have done. Jeremiah's despair was even greater than David's as he preached for a lifetime while his countrymen ignored him. The old prophet suffered because of the Jews' hardness of heart, even though he was faithful to the Lord. David and Jeremiah entered the valley for different reasons, yet both of them could see God's hand directing the course of their lives. Neither one stumbled into the place of darkness by accident. God led them there.

It is frightening to think that the path God takes us down may lead right through the middle of our nightmares. Yet knowing the Lord brought us to this dark and gloomy place is the first key to surviving it. If we could have slipped away from the Shepherd and made our own way into this place, we would face it alone. The steep canyon walls, the dark, the cold would be ours to endure all by ourselves. But we never enter the valley on our own, nor are we ever abandoned in the midst of it. The promise of Psalm 23:4 is this: The Lord will never lead us into the darkness only to desert us. David said, "I will fear no evil, for you are with me." Every step of the way, in the darkest corners, "You are with me." His words express an absolute certainty. He doesn't say, "I believe You are with me," or, "I hope You are with me," but, "I know You are with me." If there was any doubt, the fear would overwhelm me. But I will fear no evil for I know God is right beside me.

The certainty of David's declaration gives those of us who are weak a great deal of comfort. In the midst of the valley, our faith begins to falter. Questions flood our mind, and the problems at hand so demand all of our attention that we often do not have time to run and consult our favorite Bible promises. If the comfort we derive from the presence of the Lord in times of trouble depended on the depth of our faith, most of us would be in trouble. But nothing in this passage implies God's presence is in any way dependent upon our ability to believe. For those of us who have believed, that is, those who have placed our faith in Christ, He is with us regardless of how much we believe it. We don't have to be strong; we don't have to feel particularly spiritual. He promises to be with His children in the midst of the valley.

But how do we know He is really there? After all, He is invisible. Although He spoke to people like Abraham and Samuel in an audible voice, I've never heard Him speak. Testimony services are filled with people talking about how they "felt the Lord's presence," but He has never physically pressed His hand into mine. In fact, He does not normally employ any of the natural methods human beings use to make their presence known. How then do we know He is with us when we need Him the most? The answer doesn't depend upon us. Rather, it flows out of the faithfulness of God to His Word and to His children. There are times that the valley grows so dark, so cold, that we wonder where He has gone. Yet He finds ways to let us know beyond a doubt that He is with us.

He often chooses to make His presence known through people. Earlier I spoke of the voices that rain down on us from above. Many of them sound a lot like Job's comforters who were full of advice, but lacked compassion. I don't want people like this around when I am hurting. But He sends others our way at just the right moment who almost seem like angels from heaven itself. They don't necessarily give us great words of wisdom. More than anything, they come and remind us that God loves us by letting Him love us through themselves. They listen, without swapping old war stories. They allow us to vent our real emotions without making us feel guilty for being human. They love us unconditionally and ache for us because our pain is so deep. When they walk away they leave us refreshed, able to survive one more day on the valley floor.

The Lord often chooses to speak through music. Several years ago I reached the lowest point of my ministry. A problem within the church escalated, and I had to take action. This problem had nothing to do with personality differences or any of the other things that often cause minor disagreements within a church. Instead, sin had invaded the body, and something had to be done to stop its spread. But when I took action, everything blew up in my face. At the time I truly believed my ministry in that church was over, and I doubted whether I ever wanted to pastor again. In that moment of darkness the Lord spoke through Steve Green and his song "Find Us Faithful." The trial didn't end immediately, but I knew I didn't face it alone.

The Lord also draws near to us through His Word. He often focuses our attention on one of His promises, reminding us that He hasn't forgotten about us. Sometimes the Lord chooses to speak through an episode in the lives of one of the characters in the Bible. The stories of Elijah or Paul or Christ Himself comfort and reassure us. In the valley God's Word can come alive and become the lifeline that keeps us from losing our way.

Before we move on, let me say one thing to those who are in the midst of the valley: There are times that the valley grows so dark that we don't feel like reading the Bible or praying, or doing anything else for that matter. All we can think about is our child in the hospital bed or the uncertainty of the future. We open the Bible, but our eyes cannot force the words to soak into our hearts. If you are in that state, don't feel like some sort of backslider. Our Shepherd understands what you are going through. That is one of the reasons He placed His Spirit inside us. When we cannot pray, when we cannot read His Word, when we cannot do anything but hurt, His Spirit intercedes for us with groanings words cannot express (Romans 8:26).

It is this same Spirit who reassures us that He is with us. His Spirit bears witness with our spirit that we belong to Him and that He is beside us (Romans 8:16). Like I said at the beginning of the chapter, this doesn't always feel like a particularly religious experience. Angels don't sing in our ears, nor are we bathed in an overwhelming sense of peace and joy. Yet somehow we know He is there. We know He is with us. For this reason, the Twenty-third Psalm means very little to those who have not trusted in Christ as their Savior. He could be close to them like a Shepherd with His sheep, if they would only repent and turn to Him by faith. All they need to do is call, and He would be there. Until they call, until they come to Christ, He is not. But to those who know Him, He will always be with us. God has said, "Never will I leave you; never will I forsake you" (Hebrews 13:5). There is no need to be afraid.

Many things for us to fear lurk in the darkness. Nothing is certain in the valley of the shadow. We don't know how things will turn out. We don't even know if we will survive. When David said, "I will fear no evil," he wasn't trying to make the rest of us look bad. Fear is a natural response to a situation that is larger than we are. I'm sure David's knees knocked when he realized the reports of Goliath's massive size were not exaggerations. He knew the taste of fear.

Yet his words in the Twenty-third Psalm are not the ancient equivalent to a "No Fear" T-shirt. He doesn't say that he will not be afraid no matter what may come. Nor is the phrase "I will fear no evil" another way of saying "nothing bad will happen to me." Rather, David says he will not fear *evil* for the Lord is with him. During the dark period of David's life that we explored earlier, he was forced to flee for his life from Absalom. As he fled David told Zadok the priest, "If I find favor in the Lord's eyes, he will bring me back and let me see it [the ark of the covenant] and his dwelling place again. But if he says, 'I am not pleased with you,' then I am ready; let him do to me whatever seems good to him" (2 Samuel 15:25–26). David had no guarantees about the future. As far as he knew, he would die in a matter of days. Yet he did not panic. He was willing to accept whatever the future might hold because he knew the Lord held the future. Whatever he faced, he knew God's grace would be sufficient.

Walking through the valley of the shadow of death is a frightening experience. Yet the fear that sweeps over us does not overwhelm us. With the Lord as our Shepherd we know that no matter what may happen, He remains in control. This knowledge doesn't always take away the knots in our stomachs or make us any less nervous as we wait for the surgeon's report. Fear may come, for evil is all around us, but the Lord reassures us that He is greater than anything we may face. Evil and the darkest of all trials have no power over us. It is the evil itself we will not fear, rather than the possible occurrences of bad things.

Walking through the valley usually doesn't feel like a religious experience. It does not seem particularly spiritual, moving, or life-changing. Nothing about it feels like the stuff of testimony services, at least not while the valley walls still surround us. But once the walls give way, and we finally escape the valley floor, we can look back and understand that God is always true to His promise. Even though we walk through the valley of the shadow of death, we need not fear evil, for He is with us.

NOTE

1. Genesis 12:6 uses the same Hebrew construction, "Abram traveled through the land as far as the site of the great tree of Moreh." Yet Abraham wasn't passing through Canaan on his way somewhere else. Rather, he traveled about in the midst of the land, viewing all that God had promised him. The Septuagint (the Greek translation of the Hebrew Bible from the third century before Christ) rendering of Psalm 23:4 reinforces this fact by using the phrase "Even if I should walk in the midst of the valley of the shadow of death."

Chapter Seven

YOUR ROD AND YOUR STAFF, THEY COMFORT ME

*O*n August 2, 1961, a Soviet SS-6 rocket lifted off from the Baikonur Cosmodrome and blasted into history. Tucked away in the Vostok II space capsule was Major Gherman S. Titov, the second man to orbit the earth and the first man to experience motion sickness in space. Four years after the Russian satellite Sputnik triggered the space race and six months before John Glenn would become the first American in orbit, Major Titov set out on a journey of discovery. He spent twenty-four hours and fifty-nine minutes in space, circling the globe seventeen times, all the while looking for something no human eye had ever seen. Moving faster than five miles per second, he looked out *Eagle*'s portholes, only to see nothing more than the brilliant blackness of space and the piercing light of the stars. Conspicuously missing from the picture was the most famous inhabitant of the heavenly realm. Staring out into space, Titov said, "I am high in the sky, and still I do not see the face of God."

Gherman Titov spent a day in the heavens and found them to be empty, just as he expected.

If he could have flown even higher, reaching to the far reaches of space, Titov's search would have yielded the same result. Today the Hubble telescope gives us a glimpse of the far reaches of the universe. Even though it reveals breathtaking pictures of galaxies expanding and stars exploding, it has yet to catch a glimpse of the Almighty. It's not that heaven is vacant. Rather, Titov and all the other skeptics are searching for something they will never see. Something they cannot see. God warned Moses that no eye can see the face of God, the full glory of the Almighty, and live. His essence is far beyond our limited understanding, His glory much brighter than our sinful selves. One glimpse of Him and we collapse in death, just as Uzzah did when his hand touched the ark of the covenant (2 Samuel 6:6–7).

Yet something deep inside of us would like to hitch a ride on Titov's rocket and join him in his search. The earth can be a very lonely and fearful place. We need some reassurance, some sign, that we aren't alone in this endeavor. The Bible lies before us, and we believe it to be the Word of God, but sometimes the ink on the pages is not enough. One small glance of God in His wonder would do it. All we want is a message from heaven that tells us individually, "I haven't forgotten about you. I'm still on My throne, and I still care for you."

Fortunately for you and me, we don't have to join the crew of the next space shuttle to find tangible evidence of God's love and care for us. David found it as he quietly reflected on the events of his life. Throughout the roller coaster of highs and lows, David saw it. Whether he was fighting the giant Goliath, ruling the nation, or running for his life, one constant was always there. No matter what happened to him, David could write to God, "Your rod and your staff, they comfort me." David wasn't describing literal pieces of wood in the hands of the Almighty any more than he foresaw space travel when he wrote, "If I go up to the heavens, you are there" (Psalm 139:8). To him the proof of God's presence was just as real as if he had ridden off into the sky and seen the face of God. In fact, a ride on Titov's rocket couldn't have brought David any greater comfort. His life was evidence that the Lord, like a Shepherd caring for His sheep, constantly intervenes in the lives of those He loves.

A shepherd's rod and staff were the primary tools with which he cared for the flock. The rod was usually a short club about thirty inches in length with a tapered handle. Its size made it an effective weapon for protecting the flock from predators. Shepherds also used their rods for keeping track of the sheep. At the close of the day when the sheep returned to the pen, they passed under the shepherd's rod as he counted them. With time the Hebrew term translated "rod" became synonymous with the authority of the king. The term translated "staff" that David uses in the Twenty-third Psalm referred to a long walking stick. Some staffs had a crooked end that shepherds used to lift sheep out of dangerous situations. Staffs were also used to keep the sheep on track as the shepherd led the flock.

David chose to describe God's actions by comparing them to the shepherd's rod and staff, because the Lord does for His flock what shepherds in the hills of Judea did for theirs. He protects us, guides us, rescues us, and reassures us that we belong to Him. Sometimes subtly, sometimes spectacularly, He is always at work in the lives of those who love Him. His actions make His presence unmistakably clear. They are truly His rod and staff. Through them He reassures and comforts us when we need it the most.

When we think of God's intervention in our lives, we usually think of His protection. Most of us have a story to tell of some tragedy that could have been, but was not, thanks to the Lord's action. Years later we still remember it as if it happened yesterday. Luke wrote with this same excitement in the last chapter of the book of Acts as he related one of the most amazing stories in the New Testament. Shortly after Luke and the apostle Paul were shipwrecked on the isle of Malta, Paul gathered an armload of brush for a fire. As he dropped the sticks into the flame, a viper attached itself to his arm. But the serpent's poison had no effect. Paul calmly shook the viper into the flame as if nothing had happened. And nothing did, thanks to God's intervention.

I've never had a poisonous snake attach itself to my arm (and I hope to keep things that way), but I have experienced the Lord's protection in ways that amazed me just as much as the islanders of Malta were amazed by Paul. Several years ago the hand of God reached out and caught my infant daughter as she slipped out of my arms and fell toward the floor of the church nursery. We were both bundled up for the cold. I wore an overcoat over my suit, and she was wrapped up in some sort of pink, fuzzy full-body infant coat. As I walked toward the door of the nursery, she suddenly leaned back and disappeared from my arms. Before I could move, she did a backward flip and landed face down on a crib mattress, unhurt. My wife had to drive us home, I was so shaken by the thought of what could have happened if I had been a few inches farther from the crib. God's hand did not materialize out of thin air, but His protection sovereignly oversaw the event and made sure that she wasn't hurt.

The Lord's rod and staff aren't usually so obvious. Nor do they always do what we hope for. Sometimes the viper's bite is fatal; sometimes the fall leaves permanent injuries. God's protection doesn't exempt us from every bad experience we could possibly face. The same Paul who calmly shook the viper into the fire was also flogged by Roman soldiers, given thirty-nine lashes by the Jews, stoned by an angry mob, shipwrecked, imprisoned, and beaten with rods. Yet he never complained. He never questioned God's goodness or His power. Instead he boldly confessed shortly before he died a martyr's death, "The Lord will rescue me from every evil attack and will bring me safely to his heavenly kingdom" (2 Timothy 4:18).

The Lord's protection assures us that no matter what may happen to us, He will rescue us and bring us safely to the place He has prepared for us in heaven. He will never leave us in our distress but will use everything for our good and His glory (Romans 8:28). This world has no power over those who have lost their lives to Christ. Once we are crucified with Him, not even death can affect us. Jesus conquered the grave on the day He walked out of the tomb, so what can possibly harm us now?

The Lord's rod and staff not only protect us; they also guide us. Shepherds used their staffs to keep the flock in line as they traveled through the wilderness in search of food and water. Sheep have a natural tendency to stray. One or two always find a way to slip away from the rest of the flock, with disastrous results. Shepherds in the ancient Near East searched for the lost sheep until they found it and brought it back to the fold. Many times the shepherd used his staff to lift the lost lamb out of briars or other sorts of predicaments it got itself into.

Even the shepherd with the most wayward flock had an easier time of it than the Lord has with us. We love to wander away, even if we don't go far. One week we forget to pray. Another week we misplace our Bible and don't realize it until Sunday morning rolls around. Telling others of our faith seems like a great idea when the Bible study leader brings it up, but it's funny how it completely slips our minds while sitting in the break room Thursday afternoon with a group of coworkers. We struggle to live our lives with a constant awareness of the majesty of the Lord, especially with all the distractions this planet provides. It's not that we fall back to our old way of life. We simply get sidetracked. The Lord guides, but we aren't paying very close attention.

Before we get too far away, the Lord's staff pulls us back to Him. He has too many places for us to go, too much planned for our lives, to leave us wandering around in the briars. His staff pulls us back and points our eyes to the path He blazes for us. Most of us have felt its gentle nudge. The Shepherd makes sure we do not ignore it. Many times His staff pulls us through the convicting voice of the Holy Spirit inside our hearts. Other times He chooses a human instrument, like a pastor or a close friend. In the Old Testament the Lord once used a donkey to speak to a prophet. I've never heard a donkey talk, but I have heard the Lord speak through a song on the radio or a report on the news. There's no mistaking the distinctive feel of the wood of His staff.

The Lord corrals us with His staff in order that He might set the direction of our lives. We usually take too much credit for our role in this process. Because He calls us to follow Him, we sometimes think that our primary goal is to unlock the mystery of where He wants to take us. My bookshelves don't have room for all the books written on "discovering the will of God." I believe we make this far more mysterious than it really is. Shepherds made sure their sheep knew where they were going. They used their staffs to keep the flock on track. God is not different. The psalmist calls us to delight ourselves in the Lord and commit our way to Him (Psalm 37:4–5), and then he says He will guide us.

As God intervenes in our lives, He speaks to us with something that goes beyond words. Through His rod and staff we hear the message our ears longed for, a message that reassures us He loves us and cares for us. But He doesn't stop there. The mighty Lord of the universe communicates Himself to His children. He doesn't just tell us that He loves us; He overpowers us with His love. He doesn't just tell us He will be with us; He manifests His presence in our lives. The Bible tells us what He is like, and it relates stories of what He has done in the past, but we struggle to absorb all the details. Through His rod and His staff, His intervention in our lives, He makes His Word come alive and He impresses upon our souls what our minds alone could never comprehend. As He acts,

He speaks in a way that is unmistakable and awe-inspiring. But what else would we expect from the One whom John called the Word made flesh (John 1:1, 14)?

The Shepherd speaks to His sheep by revealing different aspects of His character to us at just the right moment. For years I have understood that our God is a just God. He defends the cause of the powerless and will not tolerate evil. With justice He rules the earth and will someday judge everyone who has ever lived. I understood this doctrine to be a key attribute of God. From time to time, I even worked myself up into a lather preaching about the great justice of our God. I knew the doctrine. I understood the concept. I believed it to the core of my being.

And then one day a man died, a man who had never personally accepted Jesus Christ as his Savior. I was asked to preach his funeral. This wasn't the first time I had officiated over the funeral of an unbeliever. Looking into the casket at the deceased, my spirit recoiled at the thought of where he was now. I knew I couldn't offer any real hope to the family, which made me incredibly sad. Faced with such unpleasantness, I resorted to the Scarlett O'Hara defense mechanism: I thought about something else. This worked for a while (it has always worked for me in the past), until a child came and asked me, "Is my grandfather in heaven?" I don't know what you would say, but the only thing I could think of was, "He's in God's hands now."

My answer satisfied her, and I started to go back to thinking about something else when my words began to pound in my head. I was overwhelmed with the thought that this man truly is in the hands of the just God. His eternal destiny rests with the One who loved Him so much that He gave His only Son to die for Him. The One who is holy and just and righteous will indeed do the right thing, the just thing, with this man. Whatever He does, whatever this man's ultimate fate, the mighty Shepherd will be glorified and praised.

In that moment the Lord overwhelmed me with the beauty and wonder of His justice. He opened my eyes to see this as more than a doctrine about God—it is a revelation of the Lord Himself. He is the just One, the holy One, the One who will always do that which is right and pure and holy. Whatever He does, no one can find fault with Him. The eternal destiny of a little girl's grandfather doesn't rest in my hands, but in the hands of the loving and just God. Maybe the idea doesn't do much for you, but it brought me great comfort both at that moment and later as I faced the deaths of people I know and love, people who have never publicly followed Christ. God will do the right thing. The just thing. He will do that which brings Him praise, honor, and glory. This truth that I had known so long came alive as God revealed Himself through it.

This is why the Lord's rod and staff bring us comfort. David isn't describing some sort of theoretical or mystical concept. He understood from experience that God is deeply involved in the daily affairs of those who love the Lord. We feel the touch of His rod as He intervenes in our lives. We hear Him speak as He makes His presence known to us in tangible ways. Our eyes will never see Him in this life, and our hands will never physically feel the warmth of His touch. That doesn't mean He has forgotten us. Quite the contrary. He is here, and He is not silent. When we listen for His voice, we do not hear dry, academic concepts but the living Word, the very presence of God.

His rod and staff reassure us that He is always faithful to His children. At times we feel as if God has forgotten us. David himself cried out in the Tenth Psalm, "Why, O Lord, do you stand far off? Why do you hide yourself in times of trouble?" I've felt like that. You probably have too. And if you haven't, you will. All of us will at one time or another experience a pain so deep, a loneliness so overwhelming, that we wonder where God is hiding. His rod and staff, His intervention and the distinctive voice of His Spirit, reassure us that He is not far away. The Lord is close to the brokenhearted, David wrote in the Thirty-fourth Psalm; He saves those who are crushed in spirit. As we remember specific times and events when He has been faithful to us in the past, we know that He will be faithful today and tomorrow and forever.

He is faithful because the presence of His rod and staff in our lives is evidence that we belong to Him. Just as shepherds in the ancient Near East counted their sheep by making them walk under their rods, the Lord constantly reminds us that we are His. We belong to Him and will continue to belong to Him because of the great price He paid for us through the cross of Christ. His grace, not our performance, is what saves us and keeps us saved. At times a shepherd had to use his staff to discipline a wayward sheep. The sheep never enjoyed the act of discipline, yet it was a reminder of how much he meant to the shepherd. God disciplines us for the same reason. He is treating us as sons, as those who belong to Him.

If we will listen we will also hear Him reminding us

to be patient, to wait on Him. The Lord never gets in a hurry, yet He is never late. His timing is always impeccable. We usually forget this and charge ahead, trying to make things happen *now*. The Shepherd never lets us get too far away before we feel the distinctive pull of the crook of His staff pulling us back. In the Twenty-seventh Psalm, David wrote of evil men advancing against him and his enemies surrounding him. Rather than panic, he wrote, "Even then will I be confident. . . . Wait for the Lord; be strong and take heart and wait for the Lord" (Psalm 27:3, 14). With God, timing is more important than speed. He will never be late. He always acts at just the right time to bring the maximum glory and honor to His name.

We don't have to understand what God is doing or why He is doing it. His rod and staff calm us and comfort us with the knowledge that we can trust Him fully. We see all this best in hindsight. Only then can we see what should have been so obvious when we wondered where He was. But it is not obvious, at least not to most of us— until we look back. Then we can see His rod and staff. Protecting us. Guiding us. Disciplining us. Speaking to us. Comforting us. Hindsight is the best lens to look through because our expectations of what God should do cloud our sight in the present. He rarely does what we expect, but He always does what needs to be done for our greatest good.

Through it all He calls us to trust Him. David chose a unique term to describe the shepherd's staff. It is not the usual word in the Old Testament for a staff. The root of the word means to lean on, to trust completely. He used the same word in 2 Samuel 22:19, "[My foes] confronted me in the day of my disaster, but the Lord was my *support*" (italics added). God's rod and staff intervene in our lives, they speak to us with truth too deep for words, and they meet our greatest needs with perfect timing. Now they call us to lean completely upon the Lord, to make Him our sole support.

I don't know how a Russian cosmonaut would have responded if he had actually caught a glimpse of God in the heavens. But I do know how you and I must respond to the hand of God in our lives. He has proved Himself trustworthy. Now He calls us to entrust Him with our lives.

Chapter Eight

YOU PREPARE A TABLE

IN THE PRESENCE

OF MY ENEMIES

Stephen dined there. Bold. Confident. Calm in the midst of chaos. When opposition first arose, anyone else would have toned down his message, but not Stephen. The Jewish leaders tried to shout him down, but he never had to shout back. The Holy Spirit so filled him that no one could refute his wisdom. Even when his opponents screamed threats and lies at him, red-faced with rage, he was calm, his face like the face of an angel. They eventually stoned him. The prim and proper members of the Sanhedrin rushed at him, gnashing their teeth, yelling at the top of their lungs, hurling rocks. Stephen prayed. "Lord," he asked, "do not hold this sin against them" (Acts 7:60). He never lost his cool. He never retaliated. An island of calm in a sea of hatred, he knew what it meant to recline at the table the Lord prepared for him in the presence of his enemies.

Paul ate at the table. A storm raged for days in the Adriatic, driving the ship on which he was a prisoner across the sea. The guards had already thrown every expendable item overboard (including most of the food), hoping to lighten the load, hoping to save the ship. When neither the sun nor the stars appeared for several days, all hope of being saved was lost. Panic and hopelessness settled on the passengers and crew. They all waited to die. Everyone, that is, except Paul. On the fourteenth day he urged the sailors, guards, and his fellow prisoners to eat something. "You need it to survive," he told them. "Not one of you will lose a single hair from his head" (Acts 27:34). Confident when all hope was lost, calm while everyone else panicked, in the midst of hurricane-force winds, he ate at the table the Lord prepared for him in the presence of his enemies.

David regained his strength there. For seven days he had fasted and prayed, pleading with the Lord. He refused to eat, and he refused to get up from the ground. No one had ever seen the king in this condition. Of course, no one had ever watched him beg God for the life of his infant son. On the seventh day the child died. No one dared tell the king. His grief was so great while the boy wavered between life and death, the palace servants were afraid David would do something desperate now that his prayers laid on the ground unanswered. When David finally learned the news, he got up, washed himself, changed his clothes, and went into the house of the Lord and worshiped. With joy in the midst of sorrow, hope in the face of death, David found strength at the table the Lord prepared for him in the presence of his enemies.

Bob found encouragement there. When he first lost his job, he thought his world was over. Falsely accusing him of an act he would never commit, his accusers stripped him of his job and his integrity. As the first wave of emotion washed away, he found himself in a position where he and his family had to trust God like they never had before. And they found that the Lord truly is faithful. While he was still out of work, still unsure of what the future would bring, Bob found the unspeakable joy that comes in the presence of the Lord. He and his family discovered the table God prepared for them in the presence of their enemies.

My grandmother encouraged my father at the same table as he drove her home from the doctor's office. The drive seemed much longer than the usual two and a half hours it normally took to drive from Oklahoma City to Altus, Oklahoma. Time always comes to a halt when the doctor's diagnosis contains the word "cancer." Thirty years ago that word carried even greater horror than today. It was tantamount to a death sentence. My dad struggled to catch his breath as he drove, wondering why this godly woman would have to endure such pain. "Don't worry about me," she said. "I know where I am going." She had the disease, yet she refused to fret. Her Lord spread a table before her in the presence of her enemies, giving her the confidence she needed to confront a frightful future.

The stories never end. For followers of Christ, members of His flock, they are more than stories of unusual courage in the face of impossible odds. They are not tales of extraordinary people but of God's faithfulness. Stephen, Paul, David, Bob, and my grandmother walked into the midst of their nightmares and found the Lord had done something amazing. He already had a table waiting for them, a table set with everything they would need to overcome their enemies. God doesn't play favorites. He provides the same table for all of His children when they find themselves harassed by a cruel world. Calmness when we would expect panic, hope in the face of despair, confidence when our natural strength is gone, all come as gifts from the Lord in the most unusual places.

David described this unusual place in the fifth verse of the Twenty-third Psalm, "You prepare a table before me in the presence of my enemies." He used vivid terms that lose some of their impact when translated from Hebrew into English. The table doesn't refer to a piece of furniture, but to a mat or skin spread out on the ground. The term translated "enemy" literally means one who harasses. It focuses upon the threats and abuse heaped upon us by those who oppose us. The same word was used in the book of Esther to describe Haman, the man who plotted to destroy all the Jews throughout the kingdom of Xerxes. The word rendered "in the presence of" in our English translations carries the idea of making something conspicuous, drawing everyone's attention to it. Another form of the word means a hilltop, a place that sits in plain sight for all to see. In this passage it also carries the idea of mortifying our enemies.

Together, the Hebrew terms David used draw a picture of an army standing in attack position, their swords drawn, spears ready. Most of the men are tired and irritated. For weeks they have been in pursuit of an outlaw. The longer they have to stay away from home in this wild chase, the angrier they become. As they prepare to head out for battle, a lone figure walks to the top of a small hill in plain sight of the entire army. Calmly he spreads a mat on the ground and arranges a meal upon it. Just in case anyone fails to recognize him, he smiles and waves to the crowd before reclining on one arm to enjoy his meal. This lone figure is the man the army has been searching for, the man they came to destroy. Before they can rush toward him, he calmly sets a table in the presence of his hunters. Only a fool would do such a thing . . . a fool or someone who knows something the armies do not. He refuses to run because he knows his victory is at hand.

This word picture is the essence of David's message. The Lord is the "fool" who prepares the table. He makes sure all of His enemies know where He is and what He is doing as He sets out a picnic lunch. The meal He prepares isn't for Himself, but for us. He wants to make sure we have a front-row seat to see His power in action. The table He prepares for us in the presence of our enemies is the assurance that their efforts will fail and we will emerge victorious.

The Philistines and Amorites died long ago, yet we have no shortage of enemies who would love to destroy us. Occasionally they take on human form, like the coworker who wants nothing more than to destroy our testimony. Yet the human agents are little more than tools in the hands of a much greater enemy. This fallen world and its prince, Satan himself, go out of their way to make our lives miserable on a daily basis. Their lies echo in our ears; their influence robs us of our joy. Day after day after day the influence of evil in this world wears us down like water dripping on a piece of sandstone. Just when we think we cannot take it any longer, the Lord opens our eyes, allowing us to see the table He has prepared for us. This table offers us rest while sealing our opposition's doom.

The greatest enemy the human race faces is the one from which none of us can escape. Life is temporary, but death is certain. Nothing we can do will change this fact. All the health clubs we join and the bad habits we give up only delay the inevitable. Everyone dies in the end. My first real taste of death came when I was a firefighter in Norman, Oklahoma. Early one morning I was part of the first engine company to break through a door of a house that had smoke pouring out of its windows. As we forced the door open we saw an arm. The woman who owned the house had managed to crawl to the front door, only to find the deadbolt locked with the key far away in the kitchen. Her mother tried to get to the key but she never made it. The smoke was too thick. A few feet from the first woman, I found the body of her ten-year-old daughter, along with another ten-year-old girl who was spending the night. No one survived.

What struck me about that night, beyond the horrible nightmare of four lives tragically lost because they did not have working smoke detectors, was the reaction of my coworkers to death. I was just a rookie, but the other firefighters had faced scenes like this many times before. Yet as they came face-to-face with death they became incredibly angry. Through the black of the smoke, I could hear men yelling out all sorts of obscenities. They weren't just mad. It was as though they were trying to drive death away from them. That dark night brought all of them face-to-face with their own mortality, and they recoiled against it.

For those who follow Christ, our face-to-face encounters with death have a different effect. In the very presence of the one enemy who takes everyone, the Lord gives us hope. Listen to the way the apostle Paul comforted members of the church in Thessalonica:

> Brothers, we do not want you to be ignorant about those who fall asleep, or to grieve like the rest of men, who have no hope. We believe that Jesus died and rose again and so we believe that God will bring with Jesus those who have fallen asleep in him. . . . For the Lord himself will come down from heaven, with a loud command, with the voice of the archangel and with the trumpet call of God, and the dead in Christ will rise first. After that, we who are still alive and are left will be caught up together with them in the clouds to meet the Lord in the air. And so we will be with the Lord forever. Therefore encourage each other with these words. (1 Thessalonians 4:13–14, 16–18)

The enemy of death still takes the physical lives of Christians, but it is powerless to hold us. The grave is not the end. We face it with the hope that those who are absent from the body are at home with the Lord (2 Corinthians 5:8). Moreover, we know that a day is coming when death will be totally destroyed. On that day we will take up the taunt, "Where, O death, is your victory? Where, O death, is your sting?" (1 Corinthians 15:55). Because Jesus rose from the dead, we face the grave with complete confidence and hope; it is merely a part of the table He has prepared for us in the presence of our enemies.

Another of the enemies we cannot escape is the inherent weakness that comes from being human. The winter of 1998, an infamous El Niño year, reminded us that in spite of all of our technological advances, we creatures of dust are still susceptible to the elements around us. Homeowners in California watched in desperation as their homes slid down hillsides in a sea of mud. Floods struck the Southeast, and tornadoes swept across Florida and Alabama. Every new El Niño phenomenon was another reminder that we are not nearly as strong and powerful as we think we are.

It is not just the weather that reminds us of that fact. Our weaknesses encompass every part of life. Our bodies ache after we exercise, we have trouble remembering little details as we grow older, and microscopic flu bugs have the power to completely knock us out for several days. We are weak, limited, human. Paul called our bodies jars of clay, something very fragile. Yet God takes this jar of clay and fills it with His power. As 2 Corinthians 4:7 says, "But we have this treasure in jars of clay to show that this all-surpassing power is from God and not from us." Our weakness doesn't limit God. Rather, it provides an avenue by which He can demonstrate His power in our lives. He prepares a table for us in the presence of this enemy by making a way for us to rejoice in all of the hardships, our trials, our frailty, everything that pushes us over the edge of our endurance.

Nothing pushes us to the edge like temptation. I wish that God would remove our ability to sin the moment we accept Christ as our Savior. His Word assures us that sin no longer has control over us (Romans 6:5–7), but temptation still has a way of making our lives miserable. Every day it is the same routine. A battle rages inside. The good I want to do, I too often fail to do. And the things I hate, I do all the time. Temptation never leaves me alone, neither does the guilt for the times I failed to be strong. The word translated "enemy" that David used in Psalm 23 hits the nail on the head when it comes to sin and temptation. They constantly harass every person who longs to follow Christ by faith.

The table the Lord prepares for us in the face of this enemy carves out a refuge for us. The centerpiece of the table is a promise:

> No temptation has seized you except what is common to man. And God is faithful; he will not let you be tempted beyond what you can bear. But when you are tempted, he will also provide a way out so that you can stand up under it. (1 Corinthians 10:13)

Temptation never goes away. It carefully finds every weakness we have and exploits them all to its full advantage. Yet the Lord makes sure that temptation cannot prevail over us. In the face of its assault, the Lord provides a way out, relief from the storm. He makes sure that those who have died with Christ Jesus will no longer be slaves of sin.

And when we do fail and give in to temptation, the Lord has made provision. Nothing stings like knowing we've blown it. When we give in to sin we bring disgrace to the name of Christ and grieve the Holy Spirit who dwells within us. On top of all that is the knowledge that we have disappointed those who look to us as the real deal, the picture of what a Christian is supposed to be. How could we have done such a thing? And how can God ever do anything with us again? We've had our shot, but now it's over. At least that's the line we hear from the father of lies.

Our Father has something else in store for those of us who follow His Son by faith. "There is now no condemnation for those who are in Christ Jesus, because through Christ Jesus the law of the Spirit of life set me free from the law of sin and death" (Romans 8:1). All of our sins—past, present, and future—were nailed to the cross with Christ. When God declared us righteous on the day we accepted Christ as our Savior, He meant it. This doesn't give us a license to sin. How could we who have died to sin continue to live in it? But when we do give in to temptation, we are not kicked out of the Lord's flock. He assures us that as we confess our sin, we will find that He has already forgiven it. More than that, He will cleanse us from all unrighteousness (1 John 1:9). The wonder of His forgiveness silences the harassing voice of condemnation forever.

Even when our harassers take on human form, our Lord is there. Most of us have never lived through the kind of opposition the early church endured. As soon as the story began to spread that Jesus had risen from the dead, the Jewish leaders sprang into action. If they allowed this news to go unchecked, an even greater problem than Jesus would soon envelop them. They decided to go straight to the source. The Jewish leaders brought Peter and John before the ruling council, the Sanhedrin, and warned them to stop preaching this foolishness. This same group had sentenced Jesus to death just a few months earlier, so they would not hesitate to do the same to His followers. Rather than cower in fear, Peter replied, "We cannot help speaking about what we have seen and heard" (Acts 4:20). On another occasion the Jews' threats turned into reality, and the apostles were flogged. Peter and the others rejoiced because they had been counted worthy of suffering disgrace for the name of Christ.

Peter, John, and the other apostles were not some sort of supermen. They did not possess anything we do not have. The confidence they exuded flowed from the Holy Spirit within them. The Lord empowered their speech and gave them the boldness to stand firm with the gospel. He also gave them an unbelievable peace in the midst of the turmoil they faced. Later in the book of Acts, Peter was waiting in jail to be executed. Unlike most condemned men, he did not spend his last night filing last-second appeals or pacing the floor. He went to sleep. In fact, his sleep was so deep that the angel that came to his rescue had to kick Peter in the side to wake him up!

The Lord sets the same confidence, joy, and peace before us when we face a firestorm of opposition. Jesus Himself prepared us for these moments when He told us not to worry about what we will say when we are arrested for preaching the gospel. His Spirit will speak through us (Matthew 10:19–20). We can relax, sit back, and enjoy the table He has prepared for us. Even though followers of Christ will seem to be defeated, even when members of His flock have to pay for their faith with their lives, He still prevails. The world and all of our enemies are defeated by the blood of the Lamb, by the word of our testimony, and by not loving our lives even unto death (Revelation 12:11). The strength to make all of the above a reality is found at the table the Lord prepares in the presence of our enemies.

Stephen dined there. So did Paul. And David. And so can you and I. The Lord is faithful. He always prevails.

Chapter Nine

YOU ANOINT MY

HEAD WITH OIL;

MY CUP OVERFLOWS

Who am I, O Sovereign Lord,
and what is my family,
that you have brought me this far?
(2 Samuel 7:18)

*I*t's frightening to think that we can get used to something like this, something so far beyond belief, something so wonderful. But we can, and we do. With time the wonder wears off, and we stop asking, "Who am I that You have brought me this far?" The memories of what we once were fade away, and the excitement of our new life wanes. We are still thankful and glad. We are glad we will go to heaven when we die, thankful we can call out to God at any time, relieved that we no longer have to carry around a burden of guilt. Yet we lose the awe and surprise that something this wonderful could be given to us. We get used to being saved, accustomed to life in the family of God. Like people living in the shadow of the Sierra Nevada mountains who rarely take time to stop and stare at their snowcapped peaks, the wonder of it all somehow escapes us.

> And as if this were not enough in your sight, O Sovereign Lord, you have also spoken about the future of the house of your servant. Is this your usual way of dealing with man, O Sovereign Lord? (2 Samuel 7:19)

"Is this Your usual way of dealing with man, O Sovereign Lord?" David asked. Many of us operate as if it were. Of course God saves, of course He offers a second chance. Of course He adopts human beings into His family, of course He builds us into a royal priesthood and a holy nation, of course He entrusts us with the position of God's official ambassadors on planet Earth. Of course He prepares a place for us in glory, of course He promises to seat us on thrones with Christ in order that we can reign with Him forever and ever. Of course He promises to be our God and let us be His people. Of course this is His usual way of dealing with the human race. At least it is from our perspective, from the perspective of those who have grown accustomed to His grace. Of course God redeems fallen souls. It's His job, isn't it?

> What more can David say to you? For you know your servant, O Sovereign Lord. For the sake of your word and according to your will, you have done this great thing and made it known to your servant. (2 Samuel 7:20–21)

He really should not do this. We do not deserve any of it, not even the slightest act of kindness. But God has done much more than a small act of kindness. For the sake of His Word and according to His will, He has lifted us up and placed us in a position of high honor. Yes, He saves us, but salvation only scratches the surface of all that He has done and all that He plans to do for you and me. In spite of our pasts, and in spite of all our acts of rebellion against His throne, He crowns us with glory through His Son. The thought should leave us speechless. It did David. "What more can I say?" he asked. Words cannot describe the awesome wonder of all that God has prepared for those who love Him.

You anoint my head with oil; my cup overflows. (Psalm 23:5)

When he was still a boy, David was anointed by Samuel to be king. The old prophet poured a flask of oil over David's head as a sign that God had set this boy apart for Himself and filled him with His Spirit. Yet Psalm 23:5 does not use the Hebrew word that means to anoint a king.

Because of his devotion to the Lord, David spent many hours in the house of the Lord, the tent that held the ark of the covenant. Within the tent were many vessels that were consecrated to God. The table of consecrated bread, the lampstand, even the ark of the covenant itself were sprinkled with oil on the day they were dedicated to the Lord. Never again could any of them be used for anything ordinary. As anointed vessels they belonged to God. But the term that means to anoint something for the Lord's use does not appear in Psalm 23.

As a shepherd David knew all about the medicinal value of oil. Shepherds poured oil on a sheep's wounds to protect them from parasites and speed the healing process. Oil was also poured over the head of sheep to keep flies away. The soothing ointment calmed the flock by relieving the constant irritation of pesky insects. But in Psalm 23:5 David the shepherd doesn't use the term that refers to medicinal anointing of sheep with oil.

In fact, the word David uses is translated "anoint" in this passage alone in the entire Old Testament. The term literally means to spread fat across the forehead. Throughout the rest of the Hebrew Bible the term refers to the rich blessings God bestows on those who love Him. The term also described the anointing bestowed upon honored guests as they entered a home for a banquet. Hosts would pour perfumed oil over the heads of their guests as a way of showing them honor and respect. In this way the word speaks of the position of high honor to which the Lord lifts those who follow Him. When David writes, "You anoint my head with oil; my cup overflows," he celebrates the great blessings and honor God bestowed upon him throughout his life.

> How great you are, O Sovereign Lord! There is no one like you, and there is no God but you, as we have heard with our own ears. (2 Samuel 7:22)

Why would God choose to honor you and me? He is the Almighty Lord of the universe. Our minds cannot even begin to understand the extent of His power and glory. The universe itself cannot contain Him. Everything that is owes its existence to the day He spoke a word and it all appeared. He continues to hold everything together by the same word. If He loosed His hold for just a moment all of creation would fly apart, back into oblivion.

His awesome power is only one small part of who

He is. The glory that radiates from Him outshines a million suns. It is more than light; it is the glory of pure holiness. One quick glance at His glory would destroy sinful creatures like you and me. That He doesn't destroy us should amaze us. That He would even create us is a mystery no one has yet figured out. Why would He make us in His image? Why would He choose to relate to us and allow us to know Him? Why would He make a way for us to be saved from the sin we choose? Why would He lift us up and make us members of His family? Why would the One who deserves all praise and honor and glory choose to bless us and honor us?

There is really nothing about us that would prompt God to do these things. He created us in His image, but we chose to drag that image through the mud of sin and defile it. Every part of our being is affected. We are born in sin, and apart from God's grace we will die in sin. All of the good that we can do, all the personal righteousness we can muster up, is nothing more than filthy rags. We may honor one another and sing praises to ourselves, but from God's perspective there is nothing honorable about us. Given our track record, God would be perfectly justified if He sent another flood to wipe us all out. That is exactly what we deserve; it is the reward our sin demands.

"How great you are, O Sovereign Lord!" David cried out. How great indeed. As we stand in the light of His glory, we realize how great He is and how small we are. We cannot explain the hows and whys of all He chooses to do for us. Only one word comes close: grace. The great, mighty, awesome, holy, glorious, sovereign Lord anoints us with the oil of blessing and honor out of His grace. He chooses to do that which we can never understand because He loves us. Saving us and blessing us brings Him joy for reasons beyond our understanding. The only explanation is grace.

> And who is like your people Israel—the one nation on earth that God went out to redeem as a people for himself, and to make a name for himself, and to perform great and awesome wonders by driving out nations and their gods from before your people, whom you redeemed from Egypt? You have established your people Israel as your very own forever, and you, O Lord, have become their God. (2 Samuel 7:23–24)

Out of all the nations in antiquity, God chose to place His name upon one: Israel. He made this choice before Israel became a nation, before it was even one family. The Lord began with one man and his wife, a couple already past childbearing years. He called to the man and promised him, "I will make you into a great nation and I will bless you; I will make your name great, and you will be a blessing" (Genesis 12:2). The man believed God, left his homeland, and followed the Lord by faith to the land of Canaan. There Abram and his wife, Sarai, waited for God to fulfill His promise. Along the way their names were changed by the Almighty Himself. Abram became Abraham, the father of many nations, and Sarai became Sarah, princess.

Twenty-four years later a son, Isaac, was born. Isaac had two sons, Esau and Jacob. Jacob, the younger of the two, had twelve sons who became the twelve tribes of Israel. Through these twelve sons God's promise to Abraham and Sarah came true. Their descendants outnumber the stars in the sky and the sand on the seashore. But this band of people was more than a family or even a nation. Israel was God's own possession, His own people. He placed His name upon them as a lasting testimony to the ancient world that there is one true God, the God of Abraham, Isaac, and Jacob. Unlike gods made of wood and stone, Israel's God lives, and He can be known by faith.

Israel was God's unique possession, and the nation enjoyed a unique relationship as a result. The Lord Himself declared that the Israelites would be His people and He would be their God. Through Christ this promise extends beyond Abraham's bloodline to everyone who calls upon the name of the Lord. Now you and I can be a part of this relationship; we can be a part of God's possession. The first chapter of Ephesians declares:

> And you also were included in Christ when you heard the word of truth, the gospel of your salvation. Having believed, you were marked in him with a seal, the promised Holy Spirit, who is a deposit guaranteeing our inheritance until the redemption of those who are God's possession—to the praise of his glory. (Ephesians 1:13–14)

Through Christ and by faith God gives us the privilege and honor of wearing His name. We are His people, His own possession. Out of all the nations on the earth, out of the nearly six billion people who inhabit the planet, God has chosen us in Christ to be His. The price He paid for us defies explanation. He loved us so much that He purchased our lives with the life of His only Son. Because of Christ's death and resurrection, those who follow Him by faith are His people, and He is our God.

The nation of which we are now a part stands out from the rest of the world. Exodus 19:6 declared of Israel,

"You will be for me a kingdom of priests and a holy nation." The second chapter of 1 Peter extends God's purpose for Old Testament Israel to those who follow Christ: "You also, like living stones, are being built into a spiritual house to be a holy priesthood. . . . But you are a chosen people, a royal priesthood, a holy nation, a people belonging to God" (1 Peter 2:5, 9a). God bestows this high honor on us for a specific purpose, "That you may declare the praises of him who called you out of darkness into his wonderful light" (1 Peter 2:9b).

As royal priests of the Most High God, we display God's grace to the world and invite those who are lost to experience it. The Lord promised Abraham that all the world would be blessed through him. As the spiritual children of Abraham, God uses us to make this promise a reality. The blessing we share is the blessed promise contained in the gospel of Jesus Christ. By telling others of this blessing we become like the Old Testament priests, standing between a lost world and the Lord. We declare the glory of God to everyone who will listen and plead with the Lord to save the people of the world.

As priests we also have the distinct privilege of offering spiritual sacrifices acceptable to God through Jesus Christ (1 Peter 2:5b). Unlike the priests of Israel, we do not offer sheep or oxen. The need for such sacrifices passed away when Christ gave His life on the cross. Yet we can still offer up sacrifices of praise and worship, good works, and sharing with others (Hebrews 13:15–16). The twelfth chapter of Romans commands us to offer up our entire lives as living sacrifices to the Lord. Everything we do is to be done for the glory of the Lord, in effect making everything we do an act of worship and praise.

What I find so amazing about all of this is that each and every follower of Christ can approach God with these sacrifices. We no longer need to have someone intercede to God on our behalf. Jesus Himself is our great High Priest. He has crossed the barrier between us and God so that we can approach the throne of God's grace with confidence (Hebrews 4:16). Someone as unworthy as Mark Tabb now has the distinct honor of being able to enter the presence of God at any time. Nothing about me made me worthy, nothing except the gift of God's grace through Christ.

> And now, Lord God, keep forever the promise you have made concerning your servant and his house. Do as you promised, so that your name will be great forever. Then men will say, "The Lord Almighty is God over Israel!" And the house of your servant David will be established before you. (2 Samuel 7:25–26)

David composed the song of praise to God found in the seventh chapter of 2 Samuel in response to the news Nathan the prophet gave him. Through Nathan, the Lord declared that the royal house of David would endure forever. One of David's descendants would always sit upon Israel's throne. The king didn't fully understand the wider implications of this news when he first heard it. The ultimate fulfillment of this promise came on the day Jesus was born. Matthew and Luke went to great lengths to show that both Mary and Joseph were direct descendants of David. As a result, Jesus is called "the Lion of the tribe of Judah, the Root of David" (Revelation 5:5), whose kingdom will never end.

David didn't spend a lot of time trying to solve the

mystery of how God would bring this promise to pass. He was too overwhelmed with the honor the Lord bestowed on him. As if it were not enough that God had taken him from tending sheep on a Judean hillside and raised him up to be king, now the Lord gave David an exalted name that would live forever. "Who am I, O Sovereign Lord, and what is my family, that you have brought me this far?" (2 Samuel 7:18) he asked. David understood that everything he received came as a gift from the Lord. The Almighty honored him with gifts that defied explanation. David also understood that he was not the real ruler of Israel. The Lord's people were to live under a theocracy. God Himself was the one true King. The earthly king represented God to the people. That is why David declared that through his reign men would say, "The Lord Almighty is God over Israel!" (v. 26). God ruled through the king.

The Lord has bestowed a similar honor upon us in the New Testament. Rather than setting us on thrones on earth in this life, God entrusts us with an equally important position. You and I and everyone who follows Christ by faith are God's own ambassadors to planet Earth (2 Corinthians 5:20). The Lord Himself speaks through us, imploring people to be reconciled to Him through Christ. Being an ambassador doesn't have quite the romantic ring of being a king, but He has reserved that position for His Son. Our job is to make Christ known to the world, a position of high honor He bestows on us by His grace.

O Sovereign Lord, you are God! Your words are trustworthy, and you have promised these good things to your servant. Now be pleased to bless the house of your servant, that it may continue forever in your sight; for you, O Sovereign Lord, have spoken, and with your blessing the house of your servant will be blessed forever. (2 Samuel 7:28–29)

The blessings and honor God bestowed on David were not limited by time. His kingdom was to be an everlasting kingdom; his house was established forever. The Lord Himself declared to David, "When your days are over and you rest with your fathers, I will raise up your offspring . . . and I will establish his kingdom" (2 Samuel 7:12). Death could not thwart God's promises, but it paved the way for the greatest blessings of all. When David's eyes closed in this life, God's promises to him were only beginning to come to pass. With time David's stature grew as he became the standard against which every successive king was measured. The Lord made his name great and established his reign forever and ever.

You and I are the beneficiaries of the promise God made long ago to King David. The coming of Christ and His kingdom are the direct fulfillment of the promise Nathan delivered to David. Yet we only see a small portion of what Christ's reign will be. Our hope is fixed on the day Jesus will return to set up His kingdom upon this earth. On that day all of God's enemies will be destroyed once and for all. Every promise the Lord made in both the Old and New Testaments regarding His kingdom will be fulfilled. His eternal reign will even outlast this world. A day is coming when the Lord will usher in a new heaven and a new earth over which He will reign forever and ever.

As incredible as all of the above may sound, the Lord

adds even more. Through Christ He makes us joint heirs of this kingdom. Not only will Christ reign, but those who have placed their faith in Him will reign with Him. Think about this for a moment. Allow the awe and wonder of it all to sink in. We were once enemies of God, alienated from Him by our sin. The Lord swept all of that aside at the Cross and has now lifted us up and seated us alongside Christ, and He will allow us to reign with Him forever and ever! To say our cup overflows is a gross understatement. Our Lord by His grace has anointed us with honor and glory, all because He loves us with an undying love.

He has anointed our heads with oil, placed us in a position of high honor. Our lives cannot contain the greatness of His blessings. Words cannot describe their wonder. It's frightening to think that we can get used to something like this, something so beyond belief, something so wonderful.

Chapter Ten

SURELY GOODNESS AND LOVE WILL FOLLOW ME ALL THE DAYS OF MY LIFE

*I*t is a bold statement, bordering on arrogance. From the very first word we hear it. "Surely," without a doubt, most definitely. David sounds incredibly confident, almost too confident. "Goodness and love will follow me all the days of my life." The word translated "follow" literally means to chase something down, to pursue it with dogged determination. It is a word that describes the way Tommy Lee Jones followed Harrison Ford in *The Fugitive.* That is what goodness and love will do to him, David declares. They will track him down all the days of his life. They will guard his steps and fill his life with all the blessings of the Lord.

It is a bold statement that leaves no room for doubt. The next-to-last line of the Twenty-third Psalm is not a prayer. David didn't plead with God to grant him the joy of the Lord's goodness and mercy. Instead, he saw it as a present reality, an everyday part of his life. On the hills of Judea as he tended his father's sheep, God's goodness and love followed him. Standing before the Philistine champion armed with nothing more than a sling and five stones, he was aware of God's kindness and mercy. As he sat in Saul's palace playing his harp for the king, God's blessings and grace supplied the material for his songs. While he ran for his life like an outlaw, goodness and love ran with him. Through wars and peace, victories and defeats, good times and bad, they were always there, always following David.

It is a bold statement, but declarations of faith always are. They brim with confidence because confidence is the essence of faith. Assurance. Certainty. Conviction. The writer of the book of Hebrews defined faith as "being sure of what we hope for and certain of what we do not see" (Hebrews 11:1). David's declaration in Psalm 23:6 was about far more than being certain that goodness and love will follow him all the days of his life. The One he was sure of and certain of even though he could not see Him was the Lord Himself. He was the object of David's confidence.

We can say David was speaking of his confidence in the Lord because of the words he chose. The two Hebrew terms translated "goodness and love" in the Twenty-third Psalm were used throughout the Old Testament to describe the part of God's character people appealed to in hopes of being accepted by Him. The term translated "love" is a key word the Old Testament writers used to describe God's relationship with man. The Hebrew word is *chesed,* which carries the ideas of mercy, kindness, and grace—a love that knows no limits and never fails. The word is used most often in the covenants God makes with people. His *chesed* moves

Him to reach down to mankind and enter into a relationship with us. Without it, all of us would receive the judgment we deserve because of our sin. But, as Jeremiah so beautifully put it in Lamentations 3:22, "because of the Lord's great love (*chesed*) we are not consumed, for his compassions never fail." Where we expect to find justice, God gives grace.

David appealed to the Lord's love and goodness in the Twenty-fifth Psalm when he cried out for forgiveness. The terms appear in the Thirty-first Psalm in an appeal for protection from the wicked. Psalm 54 appeals to God's goodness and unfailing love for deliverance. In the Sixty-ninth Psalm we find these words: "But I pray to you, O Lord, in the time of your favor; in your great love, O God, answer me with your sure salvation. . . . Answer me, O Lord, out of the goodness of your love; in your great mercy turn to me" (vv. 13, 16). Because of God's goodness and love, David could cry out to the Lord with the confidence that his prayer would be heard.

The Twenty-third Psalm takes this confidence a step further. Not only is the Lord merciful and kind, but His kindness will follow David all the days of his life. With the Lord as his Shepherd, David knew the Lord would continually shower him with His undeserved kindness and grace, for "he is good" and "his love endures forever" (Psalm 107:1). All those who follow the Lord by faith can share his confidence. We, too, can look ahead and know that the Lord's goodness and love will follow us all the days of our lives. Like David, our faith is based on the faithfulness of God. His love endures forever; the Lord never changes. His character and actions are always consistent. As Psalm 100:5 declares, "His faithfulness continues through all generations."

Psalm 23:6 sounds like a boastful statement. And it is. David boasted of what the Lord had done, was doing, and would do in the future. The same word "follow" was used in the book of Judges to describe armies in hot pursuit of their enemies, like hunters searching for game. David assured us that the Lord's goodness and love pursue us in the same way. They never become fatigued; they never give up the chase. All day, every day, they draw near to us as the outward manifestations of the presence of the Lord who promised to never leave us or forsake us (Deuteronomy 31:6).

The Lord's promise to be with us is more than words. He reaches down from heaven and makes His presence known in very real and unmistakable ways. Psalm 118 says it best, "In my anguish, I cried to the Lord, and he answered by setting me free. The Lord is with me; I will not be afraid. What can man do to me?" (vv. 5–6). The Lord is with me, *with me*. His mercy and kindness come down to earth and reassure us that He is right beside us. Sometimes He feels very far away. Fear and grief and anguish close in around us. But as we cry out to Him, He makes His presence known. When He draws near to us, He drives all our fear away. "I was pushed back and about to fall," the psalmist goes on to write, "but the Lord helped me. The Lord is my strength and my song; he has become my salvation" (vv. 13–14). His presence makes all the difference.

He draws near to us at the moment our strength fails. The Thirty-fourth Psalm was written at one of the lowest points in David's life. Yet he boldly declared, "The

Lord is close to the brokenhearted and saves those who are crushed in spirit" (v. 18). He knew this to be true through his own experience. In Psalm 109 he wrote, "I am poor and needy, and my heart is wounded within me. I fade away like an evening shadow; I am shaken off like a locust" (vv. 22–23). But the Lord drew near. His goodness and love pursued David so that he could write, "With my mouth I will greatly extol the Lord ... for he stands at the right hand of the needy one" (vv. 30–31). If He drew near to David, we know that He will also draw near to us as we cry out to Him.

The Lord's goodness and love also manifest themselves in His promise to forgive us. Long before 1 John 1:9 was penned, David wrote these words,

> The Lord is compassionate and gracious,
> slow to anger, abounding in love.
> He will not always accuse,
> nor will he harbor his anger forever;
> He does not treat us as our sins deserve
> or repay us according to our iniquities.
> For as high as the heavens are above the earth,
> so great is his love for those who fear him;
> As far as the east is from the west,
> so far has he removed our transgressions from us.
>
> (Psalm 103:8–12)

The Lord forgives like a loving father, full of compassion and tenderness. He doesn't drive us away or lash out at us in anger. Instead He removes our sins as far as the east is from the west, an immeasurable distance that can never be crossed. I love Psalm 103:10, "He does not treat us as our sins deserve." We don't deserve to be forgiven; we haven't earned a second chance. He gives them to us out of His goodness and grace. When we combine this thought with Psalm 23:6 we are struck by an awesome truth indeed. The Lord doesn't withhold His forgiveness, keeping it just out of our reach. Instead, He is eager to forgive His children. He takes the initiative and pursues us, cleansing our uncleanness and setting us free from the bonds of sin.

We also see God's goodness and love pursuing us in the purpose He has for our lives. Apart from Him life is nothing more than meaningless existence, a sort of living death. All of our pursuits lead nowhere, and everything we accomplish in our lives is quickly forgotten. This isn't living, it isn't life, until we find the One who declared, "I have come that they may have life, and have it to the full" (John 10:10). For members of the Lord's flock, to *not* experience a full life should be the exception, not the rule. It is not a matter of finding God's will for our lives. When we are a part of His flock, His will finds us. It pursues us, redirecting the course of our lives in order that we might enjoy the fullness of all that God prepared for us before the beginning of time.

Saul of Tarsus found the Lord in hot pursuit of him on a road going to Damascus. Up until that moment Saul thought he knew what he was going to do with his life. But on the road the Lord changed everything. Saul the persecutor of the church became Paul the apostle to the Gentiles. As he described to the church in Galatia the reason for this transformation, Paul made it clear that it was the Lord who pursued him. "God, who set me apart from birth and called me by his grace, was pleased to reveal his Son in me," Paul wrote in Galatians 1:15–16.

God's eternal purpose pursued Paul, giving him the gift of life to the full.

If God so pursued Paul while he was still Saul, how much more will His will pursue those who desire to live for Him? "For we are God's workmanship, created in Christ Jesus to do good works, which God prepared in advance for us to do" (Ephesians 2:10). Open doors for ministry are expressions of God's goodness and love in action. The opportunities He gives us to tell others of Christ or show His love in a practical way are signs that His love for us is real.

The goodness and love of the Lord pursue in places we would never expect. They also take on forms that surprise us, forms that are not always pleasant. Psalm 107 sings the praises of the Lord who is good, whose love endures forever. Yet it also tells the story of people who "sat in darkness and the deepest gloom" because they had "rebelled against the words of God and despised the counsel of the Most High" (vv. 10–11). The Lord wasn't trying to get even or exact revenge. Rather, He gently disciplined them by taking their worlds apart in order that they would turn back to Him. The writer of the book of Hebrews assures us that the Lord continues to show this same discipline to everyone who loves Him.

The promise of the sixth verse of the Twenty-third Psalm takes on many other forms. We see it in the peace God plants within our hearts. It flows through the joy that surpasses all understanding. The promises that fill His Word remind us of His goodness, and every time He is faithful to one of His promises we see His love in action. All day, every day, goodness and love pursue us. We don't have to run off in search of forgiveness or mercy or joy or peace. Our sole responsibility is to pursue the Lord. He will take care of the rest.

As He does, He gives us more than our minds can imagine. The Lord's love extends beyond His concern for our eternal destiny or fitting our souls for heaven. He delights in satisfying our desires with good things (Psalm 103:5). I find that I too often want to tone down this idea in an attempt to stay away from the theological errors of those who say God wants all of His children to be healthy and wealthy. I forget James's words, "Every good and perfect gift is from above, coming down from the Father of the heavenly lights" (James 1:17). The One who is good, the One whose love endures forever and ever, shows us how true these words are by giving us the gift of a sunny afternoon in the park with our children. He showers us with good things by giving us a quiet, romantic evening to share with our spouse. Even an occasional afternoon on the golf course with a close friend, when the thunderstorms forecast for the day don't hit until after the eighteenth hole, come from the Lord. As we pursue Him He pursues us with His goodness and grace, all because He loves us.

His love also pursues us when we walk through earth-shattering trials. Few people ever endure the nightmare that struck two sisters in Holland during the Second World War. Corrie and Betsie ten Boom went from life in the comfortable home of a watchmaker to being considered enemies of the state, women who would dare to rescue Jews from the Nazis. Their efforts landed them in the death camp Ravensbruck, hardly a place where one would expect to see God's grace and mercy. Yet one truth carried the ten Boom sisters through the experience, from their arrest by the Nazis to the death of their father in jail to Betsie's death in a concentration camp. Through it all they clung to the truth that Jesus is victor. Christ's victory transformed the death camps into a place where the glory of God was revealed through His servants. Corrie later wrote of the experience:

> Life in Ravensbruck took place on two separate levels, mutually impossible. One, the observable, external life, grew every day more horrible. The other, the life we lived with God, grew daily better, truth upon truth, glory upon glory.[1]

When I stop and consider the never-ending ways God pours out His love and grace upon me, I want to respond to Him in some way. There must be something I can do in return. But what? Maybe I should commit myself to doing good deeds for the rest of my life. I could dedicate my life to serving others or go to church every time the doors are open. Maybe becoming a missionary in the deepest, darkest jungle would repay God for His goodness and love. At the very least, I should obey His Word. There are a lot of commandments sprinkled through both Testaments. The number does not bother me; I will attempt them all. After all, God has done more for me than I will ever realize.

Yet doing good works or keeping His commandments seems so small in comparison to all He has done. For that matter, I seem so small in comparison to all He has done. I can't help but wonder why He would do this. And why would He pick me as the beneficiary of His *chesed* love, His undeserved kindness and mercy?

Or you?

Or anyone?

The Lord is good, and His mercy endures forever and ever; what can I possibly do in return? The only thing that really seems appropriate is to fall down before Him and worship Him. The daily manifestations of His kindness and love bring me face-to-face with the awesome wonder of God Himself. Who could possibly stay on his feet? King Solomon and the people of Israel could not. On the day they dedicated the temple, God displayed His glory. As the glory of the Lord filled the temple, the people fell to the pavement, their faces pressed against the ground, and worshiped Him. How could you or I do any less as God fills our lives with His presence?

As I fall down before Him, I feel as though I ought to say something. I would like to say something elegant, something that fits the moment, but the words never form on my tongue. The only words that crawl out of my mouth are "Thank You." I don't know what else to say. A pledge to give all that I own to the poor rings hollow, as if I am trying to earn what God has given. I can't earn it. I don't deserve it; I'll never deserve it. His goodness and love pursue me all the days of my life in spite of me, not because of me. Thank You is all I can think of to say in response. Thank You.

I could promise to live for Him forever and ever and ever. Come what may, I will be faithful. But that would only take me back to where I began. The faith that I so boldly declare comes as a gift from God (Ephesians 2:8–9). If He ever relaxed His grip on me for a moment, I would fall away. Sin still intrigues me. Like a dog returning to its vomit, we sinners love to run back to our folly. The Lord's goodness and grace break the chains sin held on me for so long. All I can say to Him is "Thank You."

Whoever wrote Psalm 136 faced the same dilemma. He sat and pondered all that God had done for His people, from the day He spoke the earth into existence to the day He led Israel out of Egypt. The Lord had done so much that the psalmist found himself overwhelmed. And so he wrote the simple statement, "Give thanks to the Lord, for he is good. His love endures forever" (v. 1). The same cry rings out throughout the Old Testament. Give thanks to the Lord of lords, give thanks to the God of gods, give thanks to the King of heaven. His love endures forever and ever.

Give thanks. It seems strange that we would have to be reminded. But we do. I find it far too easy to take all of the things we have discussed in this chapter for granted. God's love is so constant, His actions so consistent, that we lose track of Him. David could see the steady hand of God pursuing Him daily. I need to pray that my eyes will stay open. Only then can I assume the position I must have, a position of bowing at the feet of my Shepherd, singing His praises, giving Him thanks.

The more I praise Him for what He has done, the more I see evidence of His goodness and love in hot pursuit of me all the days of my life, the more I realize that news like this has to be told. Only a very selfish individual would hoard blessings like these. I must share them; I must tell somebody about all that the Lord has done for me, things He can and will do for them. David danced down the streets of Jerusalem singing the praises of our God. Michal, his wife, thought he made a fool of himself. And he did. But he didn't care. Only a real fool would keep silent about a God so great, so good, so loving.

It is a bold statement, bordering on arrogance. David

sounds like he is boasting, and he is. He wanted the whole world to see the glory of the Lord as displayed in His goodness and grace. Three thousand years later the Lord remains the same. You and I are now the recipients of His kindness and love. Now it is up to us to tell the world of the mercies of the Lord.

NOTE

1. Corrie ten Boom, *The Hiding Place* (Uhrichsville, Ohio: Barbour, 1987).

Chapter Eleven

I WILL DWELL IN THE HOUSE OF THE LORD FOREVER

*I*t's that last word that throws us off. *Forever.* It catches our eye and excites our imagination. Images of eternity start to dance in our head, complete with gates of pearl and streets of gold. "The house of the Lord" must be heaven. Jesus told us that in His house are many dwelling places; we cling to the hope that one room belongs to us. And we can't wait to see it. The strain of this world takes its toll. Even the greatest moments are just that, moments, moments that come and go so quickly we forget to savor them. But a moment is coming that will never pass, the moment when forever becomes today, the moment the doors open to the house of the Lord and He invites us to come and dwell there. To dwell there forever.

Yet the last line of the Twenty-third Psalm is not about heaven. David isn't talking about the place he longs to go when he dies, but the place he wants to go while he lives. He longs to dwell in the house of the Lord forever. And he does mean forever, just as a man gazes into the eyes of a woman and tells her, "I'll love you forever." David means forever in the same way a boy watching his first big-league ball game with his dad looks up and says, "I don't ever want to go home; let's stay here forever." David means forever like a mother holding her child for the first time wants the moment to never end. The king's heart ached to go to the house of the Lord, the tabernacle where the ark of the covenant was kept, and bask in the glory of God's presence, forever.

This isn't the only place we see this desire welling up inside David. It flows out of every page of the psalms. His heart beat with a passion for the Lord Himself. "As the deer pants for streams of water," he wrote in the Forty-second Psalm, "so my soul pants for you, O God. My soul thirsts for God, for the living God." In the Sixty-third Psalm he wrote of how his thirst for God was comparable to the thirst that overtakes a man in a dry and weary land where there is no water. The only place his thirst could be satisfied was in the house of the Lord, the very presence of God. "One thing I ask of the Lord, this is what I seek," he wrote in Psalm 27:4, "that I may dwell in the house of the Lord all the days of my life, to gaze upon the beauty of the Lord and to seek him in his temple."

David longed to worship God. His heart ached to sit silently in the presence of God and gaze upon the beauty of the Lord. I find that last phrase amazing. No human eye can see God, either in David's day or our own. The beauty he sought can only be seen by contemplating the wonder and awe of God. David could see it everywhere. As he gazed out on the night sky, he found himself overwhelmed by the glory of God and his own insignificance. When he studied and meditated upon the law of God, he came face-to-face with the Lord's goodness and grace. And when he entered the house of the Lord, he found himself in awe of the majesty of the Lord. Still and silent, he fell on his face to worship. He longed to stay there, forever.

I would like to say that I share David's passion with all of its intensity. Sometimes I do. A few years ago I nearly had to be drug out of the Georgia Dome at the close of the first Promise Keepers clergy conference. For three days the Holy Spirit rained down upon that place. The roof of the dome is sort of a giant Teflon tent, which is only appropriate since the glory of the Lord had filled that place just as surely as it filled the tent of testimony, the tabernacle, in the days of Moses. When the conference was over no one wanted to leave. I certainly didn't. God was there. I wanted to stay with Him forever.

Today the Georgia Dome and all that happened there lives on only as a memory. I find myself wondering how my passion for God can burn so brightly one day and hardly flicker another. But that is not the worst of it. Not only do I find my passion for the Lord fading, but I also find my motives for seeking Him become corrupt. If you and I are honest with ourselves and with God, we will admit we spend far more time seeking God's hand than His face. Not only do we lose our awe and wonder of God; we begin to see Him as a means to an end. When we call out to Him, when we seek Him, we usually want something from Him. We turn to Him in times of crisis for the strength that we need to survive. Couples come back to church and get serious about a relationship with Christ when their marriage runs into difficulties. We come to church feeling down and depressed, and we want to feel a fresh touch of His hand so that we can be happy, revived. Our motives are mixed more often than any of us will admit. More often than any of us even realize.

Unconvinced? Listen to the words you and I use when we talk about worship and church and everything else we relate to God. We read His Word in search of answers to help us cope with life. We pray when we have problems or when someone is sick or because we know that we really should pray every day. We look for churches with strong youth programs or children's programs or an active seniors group or some other program that meets a need in our life. We really enjoy church services where the music is contemporary or the hymns are traditional or the pastor tells a lot of jokes or the liturgy maintains the dignity we expect a church to have. We enjoy it unless the parking lot is too crowded or the pews are too hard, as if parking spaces and places to sit had anything at all to do with the Almighty Lord of the universe.

Do you see the problem with all of the above? Our words sound like the only thing we care about is ourselves. If our souls thirst for the living God, people cannot tell it by what we say. Most of us want the Lord only to the extent that He has something to offer us. Far too few of us know what it means to seek Him simply for the sake of losing ourselves in His presence. I don't think any of us do this intentionally. We didn't purposefully relegate God to servant status.

Maybe I am the only one who is like this. Maybe I am the only one who struggles to hush the noise of the world in order that I might hear the invitation of Christ calling me into His presence. But from what others tell me, I think many believers have trouble hearing His voice.

And He is calling. That is what is so amazing. He seeks us. His Holy Spirit draws us to Himself. The Lord God, the King of kings and Lord of lords, seeks us that we might worship Him. "A time is coming and has now come," Jesus told a Samaritan woman beside the well at Sychar, "when the true worshipers will worship the Father in spirit and truth, *for they are the kind of worshipers the Father seeks*" (John 4:23, italics added). God seeks those who will worship Him. He invites us to come into His presence and enjoy Him.

David heard the call. He heard the unmistakable voice of the Spirit of God saying to his heart, "Seek my face" (see Psalm 27:8). When he heard the Lord's invitation he cried out, "Your face, Lord, I will seek." The appetite that consumed David did not originate from deep within himself. Rather it came from the Lord. God Himself parched David's soul with a thirst that His Spirit alone can satisfy. And He continues to plant that desire within you and me today.

If we listen, we will hear the Spirit calling. The Lord's invitation to enter His presence rings out through every page of His Word. In the book of Genesis we find God walking into the Garden of Eden to spend time with the first man and woman. Later He called Abraham out of the pagan land of Ur to come to Himself. In Exodus He gave Moses the plans for the tabernacle, a place where the Lord Himself would dwell among His people. In the book of Judges the Lord sent acts of judgment designed to rescue the Israelites from idolatry so that they might worship Him alone. In the time of Solomon the Lord allowed the temple to be built in order that the entire nation might come together at specific times to seek His face. Through the prophets He called a wayward people back to Himself, while also promising that He could be found by everyone who seeks Him. In the New Testament the Lord took all of His promises a step further by sending His Son. Jesus came to seek and to save those who are lost. By doing so He opened the doors to the throne of God's grace so that we can continually seek Him.

Even when we close the Bible, we hear Him call, "Be still, and know that I am God." Not only does He call; He awakens the longing to respond. Just thinking about this leaves me speechless. Imagine. Almighty God seeks you and me to come into His presence and bask in His glory. He invites us to come to the throne of His grace, a place we have no right to enter because of our sin, a place opened wide to us because of the Cross. And as if that were not enough, He places the desire to respond within us. If left to ourselves we would continue to grovel in the mire of sin. The Lord lifts us up, seats us in heavenly places in Christ, and causes us to long to know Him more.

When we respond to Him, we find our greatest joy in the presence of God. Yet it is not a painless experience. No one can draw near to God without being confronted by His awesome holiness. There is a very good reason why the Bible tells us to fear the Lord. Anyone who has truly been in His presence understands. It is a fearful place to be. Isaiah was given the privilege of entering the temple of the Lord in a vision. His eyes saw the angels flying above God's throne, his ears heard them cry out,

"Holy, holy, holy is the Lord Almighty" (Isaiah 6:3), and his nostrils burned from the smoke of the glory of God. As his senses struggled to make sense of all they encountered, Isaiah cried out, "Woe to me! . . . I am ruined! For I am a man of unclean lips" (v. 5) Jesus' disciples felt the same holy dread the night He calmed the sea. They were terrified in the presence of the Holy One and asked one another, "Who is this? Even the wind and the waves obey him!" (Mark 4:41).

Terror in the face of God's holiness is a natural reaction for creatures like you and me. At least, it should be. He is God. We are dust. Sinful dust at that. Even after we are forgiven, even after we have plunged ourselves on the cross of Christ, we feel the dread. Not long ago in a small group of men a close friend of mine began to tell how the Lord pulled back the barrier between heaven and earth during a recent worship service in our church. He said that as he stood singing he was overwhelmed by the presence of God. My friend said that he almost felt as if he could reach out and touch God, His Spirit was so near. His reaction to the event surprised him. Entering the presence of God scared him, as well it should have.

Coming into the presence of God is a frightful experience, for it makes us painfully aware of our own sinfulness. We feel totally naked before Him. There is no place to run, no way to hide that which we hoped no one would ever see, no excuses we can make. The light of His glory penetrates every part of our souls. "Gaze upon My beauty," He calls out, but when we do we see our own hideous ugliness. We feel exposed, dirty, speechless. As long as we stay away from Him, as long as we don't let Him get too close, we feel all right. We can go to church, sing songs, even pray; we can do all of that and walk out the door just like we walked in. But when we draw near to the Lord, when the barrier between heaven and earth thins to a whisper, we not only see Him in all His glory, we see ourselves for who we really are.

That is why I wish David were writing about heaven in the last line of the Twenty-third Psalm. His words awaken a desire for God within me, but when I respond I am confronted by the Lord's holiness. My heart longs to sit quietly and know that He is God, but when I do I realize that I can no longer be in control of my own life. Contemplating the greatness of God makes my lips want to sing His praises, but as I do I understand that worship is about more than songs or emotions. It is all about being changed by the awesome wonder and grace of God. To enter into the presence of the Lord means to be changed into the image of His Son. To dwell there forever, all the days of my life, means living a life that glorifies Him in everything I do.

You and I have a choice to make. David sees to that. The same decision permeates every line of the Twenty-third Psalm. We want to read the final line as a promise, and in a way it is. All those who trust in Christ as their Savior will spend all of eternity with Him in heaven. That issue is settled. But if that is true, if our eternal destiny is to worship the Lord forever and ever, how can we be so adept at avoiding Him in this life? In the same way, how can we claim the Lord as our Shepherd if we do not constantly seek to follow Him? David's ancient poem is more than sentimental thoughts designed to stir our emotions. They testify of the life he chose to live, and they call us to do the same.

The choice we face is a choice of priorities. The Lord who is our Shepherd makes some almost unreasonable demands. *Seek Me first,* He calls out, *first and only.* He wants more than the first line in our make-believe list of what matters most in life. The Lord our Shepherd wants the firstfruits of our lives. *Seek My face,* He whispers, and He really expects us to respond, "Your face, O Lord, I will seek." He isn't looking for a cheap labor force. He desires more than a people who avoid sin. Our Shepherd calls us to so delight ourselves in Him that our greatest joy can only be found in His presence.

The choice we face is about time. It takes time to seek the Lord, it takes time to know Him, it takes time to draw into His presence. He demands our time, all of it. When the Lord is our Shepherd, our lives do not belong to us any longer. We belong to Him. Most of us want a shepherd who will protect us and feed us and love us, but the Lord is a Shepherd who owns us. Our time is really His time. The choice we must make is how we will use this time He has entrusted to us. A lot of it is wasted. He calls us to redeem it, to spend it on that which really matters, that which counts for eternity. *Seek My face,* He calls out. We must choose to make the time to do just that.

The choice we face is a choice not only about whether or not we will imitate David's passion, but about whether or not the Lord really is our Shepherd. Members of His flock, those who have tasted the kindness of His grace and the wonder of His forgiveness, cannot help but long to sit at His feet and enjoy Him forever. Their greatest desire is to draw near to Him and know

Him. Nothing the world can offer compares to the joy that is found in His presence. If the Lord is our Shepherd, we will want to dwell in His house all the days of our lives and into eternity.

If.

> The Lord is my shepherd, I shall not be in want.
> He makes me lie down in green pastures,
> he leads me beside quiet waters,
>   he restores my soul.
> He guides me in paths of righteousness
>   for his name's sake.
> Even though I walk through the valley
>   of the shadow of death,
> I will fear no evil,
>   for you are with me;
> your rod and your staff,
>   they comfort me.
> You prepare a table before me
>   in the presence of my enemies.
> You anoint my head with oil;
>   my cup overflows.
> Surely goodness and love will follow me
>   all the days of my life,
> and I will dwell in the house of the Lord
>   forever.

Chapter Twelve

OF SHEEP

AND SHEPHERDS

6:00 A.M.

Sheila slapped at the incessant noise on the nightstand and rolled over. "I'm up, I'm up," she said, trying to convince herself. "Would you go turn on the news and see if they canceled school? I think it snowed during the night."

The question was greeted with silence. She was too asleep to remember that her husband was still in New York.

6:09 A.M.

There was that noise again. The snooze button had bought her another nine minutes of sleep, if you could call it sleep. Her mind began to race with the day's activities. After getting the oldest three children off to school, she had to run to the bank, the grocery store, and the pediatrician, all before noon. From 3:15 until dinner her life would be a jumble of playing chauffeur to her kids for piano lessons, gymnastics, and basketball practice. In between she needed to run to the airport to pick up her husband and get ready for the PTA meeting she had been asked to chair. Aside from the trip to the airport, this day was basically like every other. The places changed, but the activities remained the same. Cook, cleaning lady, accountant, chauffeur. Who wants to get out of bed?

6:18 A.M.

The noise on the nightstand returned. She couldn't bring herself to look out the window. During the night she had heard sleet against her window. That's all she needed, ice on the streets. These Southerners didn't have a clue about driving when the pavement was dry, much less when a little frozen precipitation fell. They had more snow removal equipment in her small hometown outside of Dayton than they had in the entire city of Memphis. Maybe the weather guru was wrong—maybe the storm veered north. Maybe Dorothy's house really did fall on the Wicked Witch of the West.

6:27 A.M.

There was a new noise in the house, a low rumble like that of a ten-year-old boy charging down the stairs. Sheila braced herself, knowing what would come next.

The low rumble burst through her door. "Mom! Mom! Guess what! Great news! I just heard on the radio that school has been canceled. Isn't that great! A day off!" The rumble passed through her room and off toward the kitchen.

"Be quiet, you don't want to wake the . . ."

But it was too late. The distinctive cry of a six-month-old baby began to build to a crescendo in the next room. Her fourth bundle of joy, the surprise she and her husband had never anticipated when they sold all of the baby paraphernalia at a garage sale two summers ago, was awake. A fourth child made the house seem smaller, and the car needed to be replaced. *Maybe someday,* she thought to herself, *if we ever pay off the obstetrician.*

6:31 A.M.

Sheila crawled out of bed and made her way to the baby's room. On the way she tripped over the Barbie doll her youngest daughter had been supposed to put away last night before she went to bed. With baby in arms she stumbled toward the kitchen, hoping to find some coffee, but finding instead the dishes from the night before. Another chore left undone. Her fourteen-year-old daughter had promised to get to them after dinner, just as soon as she got off the phone. Judging from the kitchen twelve hours later, she was still on it. Sheila loved her children and wouldn't trade being a mother for anything, but there are days . . . And this was starting out like one of them.

Her life isn't glamorous. Hollywood executives never call asking for the film rights to her story. She is ordinary. A typical sheep who claims the Lord as her Shepherd. Becoming a Christian wasn't a decision she made easily . . . or quickly. As far back as she could remember, Sheila had heard the story of Christ's love for her. Every night her mother tucked her into bed with a Bible story. Her mother first asked her to think about accepting Jesus as her Savior when Sheila was eight. And she thought about it. She thought about it a lot, but it never went further than that. The evening Bible stories gradually stopped, and her mother quit taking her to church when Sheila's father abandoned them. Most Sundays her mother had to work, and when she didn't she was too exhausted to do much of anything. They still prayed at meals, and Sheila often watched her mother read the Bible. And she thought about what was in the Book, and she thought about accepting Jesus as her Savior, and she wondered if God really loved her.

One day she became convinced that He did. A friend invited her to a Bible study that met before school at her high school. A senior led the study every Thursday. As far as Bible teachers go, he needed a lot of polish. Every week he managed to turn a few words around, which always broke the seriousness of the moment. At first, Sheila went to the Bible study because she thought the leader was cute. It wasn't long before the Holy Spirit began to tug at her heart. The question her mother asked her to think about so long ago came back with a new sense of urgency. The time for pondering had passed. She knew it was time to act.

And so she prayed a simple prayer. When she told the Bible study group what she had done everyone hugged her, and a few of her friends cried. It was a moment she never forgot, even though it didn't seem as dramatic as some of the testimonies she had heard. She had never used drugs or had an abortion or joined a street gang. Most people already thought of her as a good kid, someone they could trust who possessed a great deal of maturity at a young age. As the years went by, she sometimes wished she had more of a story to tell. Instead hers was very ordinary, very typical of a member of the Lord's flock.

7:00 A.M.

The coffee made, the baby lying sleeping on her chest, Sheila's morning guests arrived. Matt and Katie and the rest of the *Today* show crew were never late. The tone of another adult's voice sounded exceptionally sweet with her husband gone for several days. Sheila thought about putting the baby back in his crib, but thought better of it. Nothing is quite as special as the feel of a warm child cuddled up against his mother on a cold winter morning.

7:03 A.M.

The first of what promised to be many minor explosions struck. When the enthusiasm of a ten-year-old boy on the first real snow of the season runs headlong into the sleep patterns of a fourteen-year-old girl, sparks are sure to fly. Snow days. A child's paradise, a mother's nightmare.

7:45 A.M.

A fragile peace was established. Breakfast was on the table, and everyone was now wide awake. With the gentle rhythm of spoons bouncing across bowls in the background, Sheila began to read aloud to her children, *"Do not let your hearts be troubled. Trust in God; trust also in me. In my Father's house are many rooms . . . "* (John 14:1–2). Her fourteen-year-old daughter shifted restlessly, trying to avoid eye contact. Although she had made a decision for

Christ five years previously, she rarely volunteered any information during the family devotions. The baby grabbed handfuls of oatmeal and proceeded to rub them across his face. Apparently food tastes better when it is worn. Her eight-year-old daughter regularly looked up from her cereal to ask questions. "Who is Jesus talking to? ...Where is His Father's house? ... Is that where Grandma is?" And her ten-year-old son was still for the first time that morning. Sheila wasn't certain, but she thought he might be thinking about Christ's claims on his life.

Before she reached the sixth verse of the fourteenth chapter of John (the main verse she wanted to talk about), the moment was lost. The baby grew tired of rubbing oatmeal in his own hair and wanted to share it with his sisters. Sheila's older son found this wildly hilarious and thought he would help his little brother. This immediately brought a chorus of "Mooommmmm ... make him stop ..." and other assorted pleas. Sheila sometimes wondered why she bothered with devotions at breakfast, especially when her husband was out of town. But she never forgot the impact her mother's Bible stories had on her, and she was determined to affect her children's lives for eternity.

9:13 A.M.

An island of peace. The baby was down for his nap; the other three children were outside playing in the snow. It took more than half an hour to find gloves that fit for everyone. Sheila could only find two and a half pairs of the snow boots she bought at the end of last winter and had to resort to wrapping plastic bags around an old pair of Reeboks for her son.

With the house all to herself, she switched off the television and opened her Bible. Long ago, in the days before children, she tried to have her quiet time first thing every morning. Now she grabbed any quiet moment she could get. Her goal was to spend time reading the Bible and praying every day, but she was lucky to have a quiet time four days a week. Lately she found herself praying more than usual. Her father had called for the first time in years a few weeks earlier. He was dying and wanted to set things right with her before it was too late. The call was a shock, his request even more so. She wasn't so sure she wanted to let him off the hook without some sort of repayment. The more she prayed about his request, the more she was surprised to find that she did not want to forgive him. The discovery frightened her and drove her to her knees, begging for the Lord's mercy.

11:05 A.M.

Three thawing bodies gathered around the television watching Bob Barker give away fabulous prizes. Sheila's eight year old sipped her second cup of hot chocolate, after spilling the first on the carpet. During commercial breaks, a wrestling match for the remote would break out. Her son wanted to switch to Sportscenter for highlights of last night's basketball games, the younger girl wanted to watch Barney, but the oldest refused to switch channels. She hated commercial channel surfing. The referee decided to let this one go. Some arguments are simply too silly for a mother to intervene.

The sun broke through the clouds threatening to melt the snow, much to her older son's disapproval. The school's schedule had three built-in snow days, and he wanted to use them all. If the streets became passable Sheila would be able to make it to the grocery store before the family ran out of milk, but she didn't want them to become so clear that she could make it to basketball practice and piano and gymnastics. Her husband had already called saying his flight had been delayed. He wasn't sure he would be able to come home today.

3:20 P.M.

What should have been a twenty-minute drive to the airport had turned into two hours. If she had known the drive would take so long, she might have reconsidered bringing all four children along. Traffic delays tax anyone's patience, especially that of three children crowded into a backseat. Sheila tried to make the best of a bad situation. At first she tried singing with the children, but only two of them would cooperate. She tried to get them to recite some of their Awana verses, but there is something about being forced to sit close enough to touch your brother and sister that makes the brain shut down any useful information. Finally, Sheila resorted to putting DC Talk's *Jesus Freak* into the tape player and turning the volume up loud. The baby slept through all of it.

9:49 P.M.

The only sound in the house was the muffled sound of a blow dryer in the back bathroom. Sheila and her husband sat close together on the couch, enjoying the silence and the first moment they had been alone together in five days. The schools announced that they would be open tomorrow. Today's pediatrician appointment was rescheduled for ten o'clock tomorrow morning.

Sheila never did make it to the grocery store. There wasn't any milk in the refrigerator, so everyone would have to settle for frozen waffles in the morning.

Sheila and Chris talked about nothing in particular for a short time, until their conversation was interrupted by the long, deep breaths of the early stages of sleep. He was exhausted from spending the day traveling. Chris's flight was delayed twice and finally rerouted through Cincinnati. A few minutes of silence was all he needed to pass out. Sheila thought about going on to bed but couldn't work up the energy to walk into the bedroom. It won't be long until the alarm goes off again.

Sheila's life is so ordinary because that is the kind of people the Lord calls to Himself. Not many of us are exceptionally gifted; most of us do not stand out from the crowd as special. We come from every race, every nation, every ethnic group. On the surface we are no different from anyone else. The only thing that sets us apart is the One we follow. He is our Shepherd. He loves us and cares for us with a love none of us can really understand. For some reason known only to Himself, He chooses to make us a part of His flock and draw us to Himself. An extraordinary Shepherd leading very ordinary sheep.

And He calls us to follow Him, to serve Him, to seek Him in the ordinary flow of our lives. Occasionally He pulls us out of the routine and sends us off on an adventure, but most of the time life in His sheep pen lacks excitement and thrills. The Lord is not our theme park operator; He is our Shepherd. He calls us to be faithful to Him in everything we do. No task is too small, no moment too mundane. Whether we are traveling to the other side of the globe as a missionary or driving the after-school carpool, our primary task is to glorify God with our lives. Most of us would volunteer to do great things for God, but that is not what He is looking for. He calls His sheep to do even the smallest things for Him.

Living as a sheep before the Shepherd doesn't give us any guarantees in life. We still struggle to make ends meet; we still wrestle with the hard commands of Christ. Forgiving those who hurt us and loving those who take us for granted are difficult tasks for even the most devoted believers. Memories of the past can still haunt us, and surprises in the present can upset our plans for the future. The Lord never told us, *Let Me make your life a paradise on earth*. Instead He calls us to follow Him and trust that He loves us and knows what is best for us.

When all is said and done, this is the core of what it means to be a lamb living in the light of the love of the Shepherd. He loves us, and we entrust Him with our lives. He cares for us, and we draw near to Him. He gave His Son to purchase us, to make us a part of His flock. We, in turn, offer ourselves to Him. He leads through the ordinary and the extraordinary, in the green pastures, beside the quiet waters, in paths of righteousness, through the valley of the shadow. He leads; we follow. He is the Shepherd; we are His sheep.

REVIEW AND STUDY GUIDE

INTRODUCTION

The purpose of the Foundations of the Faith series is to reacquaint the reader with some of the great doctrines and favorite Scripture passages relating to our Christian life. Indeed, these books attempt to link together our faith as we understand it and our life as we live it. Though our goal is to provide more in-depth teaching on a topic, we hope to accomplish this with a popular style and practical application. Books in the series include *On Our Knees and in His Arms, Enjoying God Forever,* and *The Only Way to Happiness.*

In keeping with our goal of a popular-level treatment, this review and study guide is not meant to involve exhaustive digging, but to reinforce the important concepts in the "Points for Consideration" and to help you explore some of their implications in the "Questions and Response."

A book's impact is judged in the long term, and if you can retain at least one important point per chapter and answer and act upon some of the questions relevant to your life, you have made considerable progress. May God bless your walk with Him as you enter into these exercises.

JAMES S. BELL, JR.

Chapter One

1. We tend to downplay the challenges of the Twenty-third Psalm because it seems to focus primarily on protection and blessing.

2. It contains, nonetheless, an implicit challenge to change our lives—to live by radical obedience and faith even in the midst of trouble.

3. We cannot consider God to be our Shepherd unless we choose Him over and above all other power and security in this life.

4. The image of our God as Shepherd is one of both gentleness and power, as well as sovereignty over our lives.

5. Because we have a Shepherd, we lay aside our own agenda and depend on His leading—a concept that is not natural to Christians in our country.

QUESTIONS AND RESPONSE

1. Why do you think David experienced God as his Shepherd to a greater degree in uncertainty and trouble than in instances of blessing?

2. The author said the opening line of the psalm can be disturbing. What was said in this chapter that would cause you to agree?

Chapter Two

1. Much of what we consider to be needs in life are really only wants, helping to make life more pleasurable.

2. We rarely think of God as our main need in life, yet we are made for Him and will not be ultimately satisfied unless He is central.

3. Often we allow ourselves to be satisfied not with too much, but with too little from life; we need to increase our appetites for more of God.

4. When we have truly experienced the fullness of God, we do not feel the need for other earthly things to fulfill us.

5. Those who have discovered the riches of Christ will endure any kind of hardship to stay in an intimate relationship with Him, because nothing compares to Him.

Questions and Response

1. Name some of the things in life that you often feel are needs but are really only wants. What is the danger in receiving all your wants?

2. What ways in your own life have you displayed the following characteristics of a sheep: stupidity, helplessness, and stubbornness?

Chapter Three

1. God builds rest into the cycles of our lives and expects us to cease from our labors in order to be replenished.

2. Jesus set an example by being deliberate and focused but never rushed or panicked in His activity.

3. Above all our many needs is the need to let the Lord take control of them and relax in the presence of the Shepherd.

4. When we thank God we still do not realize the magnitude of all He has given us or comprehend that everything of value is in Christ.

5. Prayer is a two-way street of talking and listening to God, who wants to hear from us and speak to us.

QUESTIONS AND RESPONSE

1. How often in prayer are you still before God? Take some time out soon to simply enjoy His presence and listen.

2. Think of a time when God made you slow down and wait. What did you learn when your own plans were thwarted from trying to do it yourself?

Chapter Four

POINTS FOR CONSIDERATION

1. The responsibilities of life may not merely cause physical fatigue but, if we are not careful, can dry up our souls as well.

2. That God will restore our dry and weary souls is a promise that we should all take advantage of by surrendering to Him.

3. Distractions of all kinds, even important responsibilities, can deplete us and prohibit us from receiving restoration and the fullness of God's Spirit.

4. Restoration can come indirectly by God using people or other channels to communicate His strength and power and bring us rest.

5. Since our tendencies are to overcommit and forge ahead in our own strength, God may pull us back unexpectedly when we don't know there is a problem.

QUESTIONS AND RESPONSE

1. List the areas of your life, good and bad, that most distract you from hearing God's voice. Take some time to be alone with God and let Him guide you to correct these situations.

2. When has God brought your life to a halt to get your attention? What did waiting and perhaps even suffering do for you?

Chapter Five

1. Because we are God's children, it is His name that is at stake (not merely our own) as we interact with the world.

2. The path of righteousness is a way of living—a standard that reflects God's moral character in all we do and say.

3. True Christianity is not a matter of God making us feel better about ourselves, but of God's love inspiring us to lay down our lives for others.

4. As a Good Shepherd, God makes our paths clear and straightforward by His Word and Spirit, giving us grace to make right choices.

5. There are times when we don't fully understand where God is leading us or why, but He has promised never to leave us and always to guide us.

QUESTIONS AND RESPONSE

1. Review the righteous acts in the chapter. What precepts or commands are you consistently keeping in terms of living a righteous life? Where do you need more effort?

2. If you wore a "What Would Jesus Do?" bracelet in the last twenty-four hours, what would you have done, said, or thought to live up to this model?

Chapter Six

1. The experience of "the valley of the shadow of death" goes far beyond ordinary trials and shakes the foundation of our very being.

2. This valley may be entered because of our own serious sin, as David endured the consequences of his sin with Bathsheba.

3. Jeremiah, on the other hand, entered the valley because of spiritual opposition, demonstrating that the Lord sometimes calls us to confront the darkness.

4. One effect of walking through this valley is spiritual dryness; yet God is still with us and intercedes for us even when we may not feel His presence.

5. Though walking through the valley may not seem in the long run either uplifting or spiritual, we can look back and see God's faithfulness in the worst circumstances.

Questions and Response

1. What in your life has been the closest experience to the valley of the shadow of death? How did it differ from other trials?

2. What might be some of the signs of God's presence in your life during an experience like this?

Chapter Seven

1. We don't need to see God to be reassured of His existence, but rather we see the evidence of His hand in the many events of our lives.

2. God's rod and staff protect us as we encounter danger that we cannot foresee, keeping us from stumbling.

3. Though we often get distracted from the commands of Scripture, God's staff pulls us back into His will for our lives.

4. Though we don't always understand God's ways, especially with trials or eternal punishment, we know the outcome contains His love, justice, and holiness.

5. The Shepherd uses His rod and staff in unpredictable yet timely and perfect ways—for our discipline, protection, guidance, and even comfort.

QUESTIONS AND RESPONSE

1. Name three situations when you were very grateful for either the rod or the staff. How did they work to set you straight?

2. When in your past did you initially resist the rod or staff yet later understand the important intervention of the Lord?

Chapter Eight

Points for Consideration

Points for Consideration

1. When God spreads a table before us in front of our enemies we can calmly accept the most difficult circumstances and know that He will provide sustenance.

2. We should not cower or hide before our enemies, because God may cause us to prosper in their very presence.

3. Though Satan attempts to harass us on a daily basis, if our eyes were open we would see God's table ever before us.

4. Our lives are very fragile and death stares us in the face, but our weakness is a vehicle for God's power.

5. There is no condemnation in Christ, so even if we fail in the presence of our enemies, God will give us another chance.

Questions and Response

1. In the midst of fierce opposition, when has God turned things around for you and given you the victory?

2. Enemies are not limited to people and can come in many forms. What enemies do you contend with, some of which may be subtle?

Chapter Nine

1. We take for granted God's saving grace, but we do not realize the position of high honor in which He has placed His redeemed children.

2. In comparison to God there is nothing honorable about us, but because He is God He can legitimately grant us exaltation, blessing, and honor.

3. As royal priests of the Most High God, we offer up our entire lives as a sacrifice to Him—by worship of Him and good works for others.

4. Just as David was overwhelmed because God inaugurated an everlasting kingdom, so we should rejoice in being able to rule with Him for eternity.

5. Being ambassadors for Christ may not be as prestigious as David's kingship but it is important in light of its consequences in God's eternal kingdom.

QUESTIONS AND RESPONSE

1. When have you felt God's special anointing power in your life to serve Him, or your cup overflowing with His blessings?

2. Write a prayer similar to 2 Samuel 7:28–29 in response to God's special calling and blessing in your life.

Chapter Ten

POINTS FOR CONSIDERATION

1. David is not hoping for goodness and mercy, but boldly declaring its reality in his life both in the present and future.

2. Because God's love never changes we can have trust and confidence that He will faithfully care for us always.

3. God "hotly pursues" us, reaching down from heaven both to bless us with His continual presence and to send us help in time of great need.

4. Fullness of life in Christ is the rule rather than the exception for God's people, because He seeks us first and has the means to achieve this goal.

5. We need to pray that God will open our eyes daily to His continual goodness and love, and we need to praise Him for all He has done.

QUESTIONS AND RESPONSE

1. Goodness and mercy can sometimes translate into compassion. How has God shown you compassion in the midst of your weaknesses, mistakes, and failures?

2. How can you in turn show goodness and mercy to others by demonstrating how God displays it through Christ?

Chapter Eleven

1. The one thing David wanted to do without ceasing was to bask in the presence of the Lord, lost in wonder and awe at the beauty of His holiness.

2. We cannot only lose our passion for God quickly but can also have self-seeking motives for approaching Him.

3. God actively seeks worshipers, and He is more than willing to give us a thirst for Him so that He can satisfy our deepest needs.

4. Terror in the presence of a holy God is a normal reaction, because we see His beauty and purity compared to our ugly sinfulness.

5. The choice God as our Shepherd calls us to make requires us to seek Him with everything we have, including our time.

QUESTIONS AND RESPONSE

1. Though you may not spend "forever" in the Lord's presence, do you spend enough time so that you truly can call Him your Shepherd?

2. What portions of Scripture, books, hymns, etc., lead your soul to thirst for God? Why?

Chapter Twelve

POINTS FOR CONSIDERATION

1. The Lord chooses many ordinary sheep to lead into ordinary situations; nonetheless, He is an extraordinary Shepherd.

2. All tasks we perform have dignity and importance regardless of how exalted or mundane, if we perform them in His service.

3. Even though He provides His sheep with strength and protection, we are still asked to struggle with the hard challenges in life.

4. When we think of bringing God glory, we think of spectacular exploits, when actually obedience in the little things is just as valid.

5. We often think we are managing our own lives with God relatively absent, when actually God is actively leading us.

QUESTIONS AND RESPONSE

1. In what ways does your life parallel that of Sheila's? How does God as the Shepherd enter into this monotonous routine?

2. Identify at least one event over the last week when God manifested Himself as an extraordinary Shepherd in your ordinary circumstances.

Moody Press, a ministry of the Moody Bible Institute,
is designed for education, evangelization, and edification.
If we may assist you in knowing more about Christ
and the Christian life, please write us without obligation:
Moody Press, c/o MLM, Chicago, Illinois 60610.